*Pretty*SAD

12 Women. 12 Journeys.

*Pretty*SAD

VOLUME III

Tanya DeFreitas

Dedication

To women all over the world, especially those who silently suffered after surviving abuse, abortion, abandonment, addiction, depression, homelessness, molestation, prostitution, rape, sickness, sex trafficking, suicide, and any other form of severe trauma.

Contents

Time to Tell

Welcome to the 3rd edition of the Time to Tell movement – Voyage to Heal. In this volume of *Pretty* SAD, secrets are being exposed and the truth is coming out The authors have taken a bold and courageous step to tell it all, so they can heal and be free from the bondage of the past.

The stories you are about to read are not fictional. They are true stories, about real women, who have endured and overcome. These stories are written in *HER VOICE*. We are not here to be grammatically correct or proper. We are not here for sympathy or pity. We are here so that we can be liberated by the truth and each woman can shed light on the dark areas of her pain and her past.

These women are connected and they do not know each other. These women are from all over the world and their ages range from young and still learning to mature and still growing. Most of these women are mothers. Some of them are married. Some are divorced. Some are single. These women are from all walks of life coming together to expose the enemy and to tell the truth.

Some of these women tell more than others and that is okay. Some are very detailed and others kept their story short and to the point. Some of the stories go back to childhood, some share multiple incidents, and others focus on one event.

Each story is the truth, from her perspective. Each woman did her very best to recount the details and experiences that have shaped her life today. Each woman in this project was silenced one too many times and for too long. It is time to tell her story, her way, and in her voice!!

She is me; I am her,

Tanya DeFreitas

Lead Author
Founder of Time to Tell & Creator of *Pretty* SAD

Pretty Girl
By Ashleigh

Pretty girl, who is to blame

Frightened girl, they don't know her name

Saddened girl, who cries at night

Distant girl, who's out of sight

Psycho girl, with scars on her wrists

Fairytale girl, who don't exist

Silent girl, without a name

Ignored girl, who's filled with shame

Faking girl, with plastic smiles

Freakish girl, from a thousand miles

Emotionless girl, can't feel much pain

Darkened girl, who brings the rain

Crying girl, tears start to flood

Psychotic girl, who drains her blood

Hated girl, who no one loves

Such a weak girl, who's no longer though

Angry girl, there is no cure

Happy girl, she is no more

Hidden girl, she covers her scars

Prisoned girl, lived behind her bar's…

"You can't conquer what you don't confront."

Journey 1

Facing My Demons - Part 2

Continued from *Pretty* Sad, *Volume 2, Journey 14*

He hit me. I was asleep and I woke up to a blow to my face, not knowing if I was dreaming, or not. I was shocked and confused, as I sat up in the bed. Suddenly, I felt hot and cold on my lip and my cheek was throbbing.

I hopped out of the bed, as I remembered he was upset. He was angry about the Facebook ordeal. He must have attacked me over that. I was a bit delirious and trying to fully awaken as my mind tried to plan my next move.

Still holding the side of my face, with my hand covering my cheek and a part of my lip, I started rummaging for clothes. I was in my pajamas. It was 1 am.

He rushed to my side of the bed and got in my face. I dropped my hand and it was full of blood. His eyes widened as he saw what he had done.

He started talking, actually yelling, but in this moment I cannot remember what he was saying to me, at that time. There was fog or a cloud in the atmosphere. His voice was muffled. I could barely decipher his words. I had to have been in shock.

Usually I pop off; I argue back and I fight back. But in that moment I had no fight left. I was done. I knew that nothing I said would matter any way. I knew nothing was going to change. I also knew that if I didn't do something to get out of the house and the marriage, this man could kill me.

Most people don't understand why women stay in abusive relationships. There was a point when I didn't understand either. Until it happened to me...

∎ ∎

I watched my mother live through two abusive relationships. There may have been more, but I only remember two. In the first one, all I remember is police lights. Bright police lights shining through the window of the truck. It was cold and I was in the truck as she talked to the police. Her clothes were torn and her face was bloody. There was a lot of blood. I could barely look at her because it hurt to see her like that.

I do not remember my age when this happened, but I know that I was no more than six years old. How do I know? Because by the time I was seven years old she was in another abusive relationship. This second one that I remember, lasted until the summer after I graduated 8th grade. I was 14 years old.

In this second relationship, I was older so I remember more. I remember they fought all of the time. I didn't like it, but I was used to it.

I learned to go into my room and turn on the radio so I could drown out the arguing and screaming. I could still feel the vibrations from the bumping, tussling, fighting, or whatever would be going on, but I would just dance to the music I listened to in an effort to create my own vibrations.

It didn't make sense to cry anymore or beg them to stop because when I did that they never stopped and no one dried my tears. No one comforted me. The bumping, thumping, tussling, fighting, and screaming became a thing. Living with abuse became my normal. My mother being depressed was also my normal.

Here I am in my forties, married, with children, facing the reality and memory of my childhood. I have reached a place in my life where I am determined to defeat the demons that have caused me to follow in my mother's footsteps. I swore I would never let it happen to me. I swore I would fight back and I'd kill him or them before they would ever kill me. And I meant it.

I meant it so much that when I realized I was being emotionally abused by my first husband I contemplated murdering him. Not only did he emotionally abuse me, but I felt like he used me. I stood by his side while he served time in the state prison. We were just friends when it started, but I was there for him. I held him down. Not because I wanted a relationship, but because he was my friend and I had an unheard of loyalty to my friends.

Our relationship evolved over the years because I found myself heartbroken from relationships on the streets. He was my comforter and my confidant. He was my safe place. Naturally and due to the circumstances, we grew to love one another very deeply.

I was faithful to him and loyal to him. I married him while he was serving the last couple of years of his 13-year prison sentence. After coming home from prison, things went well, for a little while. He got a good job, took care of the household, and we spent regular quality time with our blended family. We went to church together, prayed together, and it seemed too good to be true.

Well, it was. It was not long before he fell into drugs. I was oblivious and unaware, at first. I didn't know anything about drugs, the use of the sale of them so I didn't know the signs. Someone else brought it to my attention and I began to research it to confirm its truth.

When he cheated on me, I was devastated. I was furious inside. I started having regular dreams of going to prison myself. I saw myself wearing the orange jump suit – yea the one for crazy folks because he was driving me batshit crazy.

I had dreams of my mother bringing my children to visit me. I had dreams of living life in a cell. But before those dreams, I had vivid visions of taking a knife to his stomach, jabbing him in the belly button, deeply, twisting the knife as I looked him in the eyes and watched him bleed to death. I felt like that is what he did to me – stabbed me, in my core, and watched me bleed to death. So I was going to do it to him, literally.

Thank God I decided to divorce him instead. I thought I didn't believe in divorce, but I believed in it more than I believed in spending my life in prison. The trauma from those 10 years of my life was buried and never dealt with.

Fast forward to my current marriage, my heart had not changed. I was going to fight back and I would kill him before he killed me. This was my motto deep within, but I never thought I'd have to actually fight or that I would become the violent one.

The first time my husband felt like a threat to me I grabbed a lamp. If he came closer I was going to hit him on the head and in the face with the lamp. That was my plan in my head. Since then I've grabbed lamps, mirrors, vases, knives, and anything that was nearby to use as a weapon. The same things I grabbed I have also thrown, at him.

I have picked up night stands and tossed them across the room. I have kicked bookshelves down, pushing them in his direction, with the intent to harm him, while protecting myself. I have knocked chairs and tables over, too. One time I had two knives. I gave him one and I had the other. I was ready for war and ready to die. I told him that night that if he put hands on me I'd kill him or die trying.

I had never hit a man, until my current husband. I had never busted out a window with my own fist, until my current husband. My anger and my crazy didn't flare up and come out, until my husband.

When busting out a living room window with my right hand felt good, I knew I had a problem. I had a problem before then, but that was my wake up call. I was completely out of character and beside myself. This wasn't who I was, but it was who I had become because I let my past stay buried far too long.

What I have since learned is that the anger I felt did not begin with my husband. He triggered it and he was the brunt of it. There were times when he brought it out of me based on his own actions, behaviors, and words. But the root of it all started a long time ago.

I wasn't even in school, yet. My mother let me stay at her boyfriend's sister's house. There was a party or picnic and I wanted to stay the night with the other kids. She allowed me to. What she didn't know was that I'd be molested the night I stayed.

We were in the bed. It was me and three other girls. The boys were all in another room. I don't remember what happened first or who did what, but I know that one of the girls was older than the rest of us. She's the one who started it all.

It went from fondling with clothes on to poking and licking with clothes off. I didn't like when she made me put my head in between her legs. It didn't feel right and it didn't smell right either. But I liked when she put her head in between my legs. It tickled and made me giggle. I giggled so loud that she finally stopped, after shushing me a few times.

She started messing with one of the other little girls after pushing me away. I guess she was mad that I was making noise. I didn't know we were supposed to be quiet. I didn't know this was supposed to be a secret either. When I went to tell the boys who were in another bedroom what we were doing, while she was performing oral sex on one of the other little girls, I didn't know we would all get in trouble.

The boys told the grown-ups, right away. The oldest boy woke the adults up. Lights were turned on all over the house. The sleepover party ended. This was not the last time I was at a sleepover, however. It was also not the last time that I was fondled sexually as a child or taught others how to fondle and hump because of what was taught to me. The seed of sexual abuse was planted. It took root and it grew into a monster that would attack me, again, later in life.

Fast forward a bit. I was 12 years old. I was home alone, as usual, because my mother had to work. She was a single mother. Who else was going to pay the bills? Who else was going to watch my baby brother while she worked?

I had stayed home alone before, but this time she let my cousin come over so that I'd have company. She was working a double night shift and I guess knowing that my brother and I weren't by ourselves helped her feel better.

My cousin was younger than me though. I think she was 10 years old. But she was a womanly 10, if that makes sense. She had a full figure: large breasts, wide hips, a round behind and a *Pretty* face. She was also more advanced and mature than me. She knew what to say and how to say it. She was popular with boys.

We spent the first night on the phone with some older boys and I followed her lead. I said whatever she told me to say. Then, we'd giggle knowing it was way too advanced for our immature minds and bodies. We flirted and pretended to know things and do things that we knew nothing about.

We were sipping on apple juice, while on the phone, with two older boys. My cousin told the boys who were 18 and 19 year old gangbangers that we were drinking alcohol. They liked the fact that we were "drinkers" and they wanted to drink with us. So we planned to let them come over the next night, while my mother was at work, and we were all going to drink together.

They came over and they brought alcohol. I put my baby brother to sleep and put my pretend grown woman face on. Music was playing. We were dancing, laughing, and drinking. I had never even kissed a boy so I had no clue what to do with these men, although young, still adults, in my home. I wasn't afraid, but I was nervous. I played it off though. I was the big cousin so I had to pretend to be more mature and more advanced.

I had big, large, yellow cup. It had a mixture of juice and gin inside of it. My cousin had a big cup with Coca-Cola and brandy inside of it. We sipped our cups and we sipped one another's. The boys watched and waited.

My cousin grabbed a bottle of brandy and took it to the head. This means she drank straight from the bottle. I followed her lead. I had no idea what I was doing or what I was getting myself into. It tasted awful, and it burned my throat and chest as I swallowed, but I drank and drank and drank as the boys cheered me on. This was the first time I had ever had liquor in my life and I was gonna pay for it.

Shortly after drinking half a bottle of brandy, I didn't feel so well. I laid across the couch as the room started to spin. I felt nauseous. My head began to hurt.

The next thing I remember, is saying, "That hurt." But I barely said it. I could barely speak and I couldn't see, but I felt cool air and pain around my legs and the lower part of my body. I must have blacked out, because the next thing I remember is waking up to my mother standing over me, on the floor, yelling and screaming.

I was still not in my right mind. I didn't know where I was and she kept screaming for me to get up. I did, but I could barely stand. When I did stand, I felt excruciating pain between my legs. My stomach also hurt. I grabbed my stomach and bent over because I was hurting. My mother was now screaming at my cousin. She was on my bed. I don't even remember how we got to the bedroom.

My mother made my cousin get dressed. She was naked. I had on a black tank top with no pants or panties on. I don't remember what happened.

I do remember my mother yelling that she was taking my cousin home. Seconds later, she rushed out of the door with my cousin. Everything was happening so fast. My head was still spinning. I made my way to the bathroom. As I sat on the toilet, everything below my waist hurt. I urinated and it burned. When I wiped myself it hurt something terrible.

I had a habit of looking at the toilet paper when I wiped. When I looked this time I was bleeding, a lot. It wasn't time for my period and I was not sexually active. Something had happened. But I was not able to remember anything. I still don't remember much more than I am sharing now.

I stood up from the toiler, washed my hands, and went to check on my brother. I was babysitting when the boys came over earlier. It was now about 2 am in the morning. They had come over about 4 pm. My brother wasn't in his crib so my mother must have taken him with her to take my cousin home.

I scrambled for the telephone in my bedroom and called a guy friend. I was slurring and crying, hysterically. I told him I was bleeding. I told him I was hurting. I told him the guys had been there, my mother had left to take my cousin home, and I believed she was going to kill me when she got home. I told him I didn't know what had happened.

I was a 12 year old virgin who had never even kissed a boy. I had never consumed alcohol, until then. I drank so much that I passed out. I was unconscious while I was raped so I don't know everything that happened to me. It was the hospital who confirmed that I had been raped.

My mother was angry with me. She told my aunt and uncle. My family labeled me as "fast" and I was told that I wanted what happened to happen because I let the boys in the house. The police were involved briefly, but the boys, or young men, were not charged and I didn't receive the therapy or counseling I needed. Life just went on.

It didn't get better though. At the age of 14, I was raped, again. This time I was sober and the boy was supposed to be my boyfriend. I'll save the details, for now. But just know that I didn't get counseling for that trauma either.

By the age of 17, I was in an abusive relationship with a man 10 years older than me. By the age of 19, I was a single mother, on welfare. At the age of 26, I was married to a convicted felon. Still no counseling or therapy.

By the age of 30, I had two children and I was going through a painful divorce. I walked around carrying years and years of pain, hurt, disappointment, and baggage. I was a functional depressed person. I had been clinically diagnosed with depression, but I did what I had to do because I had to do it. I was a mother. I worked. I went to school. I attended church. I did all of the things they (whoever *they* are) said that I was supposed to do. But I was still broken, damaged, and deep down very, very angry!

I wasn't on medication because "we don't do that." *We*, being my culture, my people. I didn't attend therapy for similar reasons. I masked the issues and my pain with church. I was taught that if I prayed, fasted, and lived right I would be ok. I did all of the above and thought that I was ok.

A few years passed and I met my current husband. I had a decent job, my credit was on point. I had a newer car. I was raising my children on my own. I paid my bills on time. I had a strong circle of friends. I held it down, by myself. I called my own shots. I had a few awards and accolades under my belt, a few degrees and certificates, too. I was doing good.....on the outside.

I was doing well on the inside, too, I thought. I knew Jesus. I prayed. I knew how to fast, pray in tongues, quote scripture, and all. I was not super religious either. I knew when to turn it on and when to turn it off.

I had taken relationship classes and I had prayed and fasted about marriage. So when I met my husband I thought I knew what to do. I thought I did everything I was supposed to do, right, for a change.

My expectations for marriage and my reality are much different. Despite the relationship experience I thought I had, I had not really lived with a man. My first husband paroled from prison and we lived together for five months before he violated parole and went back to prison. Other than a few overnight guests from time to time, he was the only man I had ever lived with.

My current husband and I came together under an illusion that we had so much in common we'd be fine living together and walking out the union of marriage. After all, we were both believers in God; we prayed, we fasted, and we did everything *they* told us to do.

If there is one thing I have learned it is that marriage doesn't bring out the best, it brings out the worse. If you have ANY thing in you that was left undealt with you WILL have to face it and deal with it once you are married. I wasn't prepared to face the demons that would reveal themselves once I was married. Not only did I have my own demons to face, but now I had my husband's demons before me, as well. Together, they were a force to be reckoned with. To be continued…

"I am not what happened to me; I am what I choose to become."

Journey 2

Pretty Obvious

Throughout my childhood, I was molested. It began before I even started school. My innocence was taken and caused me to have a distorted view of how the world was supposed to be. The saddest part is that the men who molested me were not strangers. These were men who were allowed in my household. These were men who gained the trust of the adults in my household. These were also the men who said they were there to protect me. You may wonder how that could possibly happen. It wasn't hard, especially when the eyes of those who were supposed to watch over me were usually blood shot red or closed.

My mom was an alcoholic and my father developed PTSD from serving in the Vietnam War. My father left my mom with me while she was just a young teenager. I am not sure if this caused my mom to turn to alcohol or if she was already drinking. I just know I have memories of her always drinking…a lot.

My mom seemed to be drawn to men who were also drinkers. These men would somehow convince my mom that it was best for them to move in with us, to take care of us. Imagine that! From the first boyfriend to the last, they would comment on how *Pretty* I was. My mom would be proud of them for saying that sometimes, but other times she would get mad and take it out on me. See, I did not resemble my mom, at all, or anyone else in my family for that matter. I stood out like a sore thumb and sometimes it would hurt my feelings, especially since I looked like my father who had left us. Nevertheless, this should have been a red flag for my mom, but it wasn't.

The first man who molested me supplied my mom with as much alcohol as she wanted. She would drink herself to sleep leaving me vulnerable and exposed to the predator within our home. He began molesting me when I was around four years old. My mom had no clue, or if she did, perhaps she became so dependent upon alcohol that she did not have the emotional strength to do anything about it.

As I got a little older, my mom and I moved in with my grandparents who were very old. The first boyfriend was no longer with us. I suppose he got tired of dealing with my mom and her drunkenness, or maybe it was because of something else. I am not sure. I just remember being glad when he left.

Moving in with my grandparents wasn't much better. They were very kind people who believed in helping other people, especially family. They would allow family members to live with us all the time.

We lived in a huge house, which was common during that time period. The same people that they were trying to help were some of the same people who molested me. My mom also had several different boyfriends who would live with us and also molest me or attempt to molest me. It just seemed that she was drawn to those types of men, especially when she became a full blown alcoholic. She would not seek help and she became angry and violent all the time.

I can recall one time that my mom took me with her to this man's house. She left me in the front room of his house while she went with him to a different room. I never saw what they did, but her demeanor was different when she came back out. I never asked her about it out of fear that she would get mad and beat me as she often did when she was drunk. She would call me names, such as, "a little *Pretty* bitch." I was her child! Yet, in her mind, I was her enemy. It wasn't always bad, but there was way more bad than good, for sure.

I was a teenager when I finally broke free of my mother's grip of terror and beatings. My grandparents also got tired of my mom's drunkenness and put her out of the house. By this time, the molestations had stopped, but I had been raped, twice already. I became emotionally detached from my family and from myself. I felt that no one was capable of protecting me and I was angry all the time.

As an adult, I sat down with my mom and had a very hard conversation. What I found out was that mom had been molested and raped, as well. She was raped as a teenager, before having me, and left in an alley to die. She was molested by family members. She drank to hide her pain rather than seeking help. I shared with my mom how her boyfriends molested me throughout my childhood. She was angry and hurt, but not enough to stop drinking. However, I told her that I forgave her, as well as the men who had hurt me.

I was an angry woman for a long time, but God saved me. He gave me a newfound love for my mom and my life. He helped me to overcome the things that happened to me. I sought help and I vowed that I would be the very opposite of my mom.

Before I ever had children, I asked God to help me to be the best mother I could be to them and to always have a watchful eye to their needs.

I sat down with my husband and told him what happened to me as a child and teenager. I strive to be a very good wife to my husband and when the time comes, to be a wonderful, trusting grandmother to my future grandchildren. If a child tells me something, I do not take it lightly. I listen and if necessary, take action.

There is no such thing as "what happens in our house stays in our house" in my home. I told my children that if someone is hurting them, in any way, to tell me because I will protect them. They are adults now, but we still have open adult conversations about love, pain, hurt or whatever. I want them to know that I will always be there for them no matter what because I know how it feels when there is no one there for you and that's *Pretty* sad.

"My flesh and my heart may fail, but God is the strength of my heart and my portion forever."
Psalm 73:26 NIV

"It's not what you are that holds you back;
it's what you think you are not."

Oh Brother

He touched me. It had been years since a man had touched me. It felt good as his hand rested on my back, while I rested on my pillow. I trusted his hand and I trusted him. He was the only man that I trusted.

Every man I knew up to this point in my life had broken my trust. They all let me down. My grandfather, my father, my uncles, my first husband, my Pastor, and every ex I had – they ALL let me down.

He was the last man standing. I admired him and looked up to him. I loved him so much and he loved me, too. He looked out for me, he checked on me, he put money in my pocket, he helped me with my children, he helped me around the house, he cooked for me, and he rubbed my feet. No man had ever rubbed my feet.

We were in my bed. It was a Queen sized bed pushed against a wall. He was laying on the inside, closest to the wall, and I was closest to the edge of the bed. It was not unusual for us to lay in the same bed. We'd lay, talk, tell stories, and laugh. He'd entertain me with stories and jokes until I felt sleepy, then he'd leave the bed and my bedroom. On this particular night, he never left.

We had both been sipping on alcohol. I was not a drinker, but I'd sip from time to time. I had recently started sipping more, with him, however. I saw no harm in it. I didn't drink to get drunk. I only sipped because it gave us something to relate and we would have some of our greatest conversations in those moments.

We were both a little tipsy. I was also physically exhausted. I had worked all day, my cycle had started and it was extremely heavy. My head on my pillow was reassuring. His presence was comforting.

I was laying on my left side with my back towards him. He was also laying on his left side. There was distance between us, as there should have been. He had been on his cellphone messaging his child's mother.

We were talking and laughing about something and I remember dozing off a bit. Then, I felt his hand touch my shoulder. I opened my eyes in the dark room. He gently rubbed my shoulder, as his hand moved towards my mid-back. He continued rubbing.

I didn't think anything of it. In fact, I enjoyed it. I had never had a massage before and if this was anything remotely close to how they felt I wanted one.

He rubbed and rubbed as I lay there, in and out of sleep. At one point, his hand stopped moving. It was positioned on my right side. He slowly slid his hand under my night shirt. I had on pants, socks, and a head scarf. I was dressed completely appropriate in my bed.

His hand was now touching my skin. It was soothing and comforting. Looking back, I think he was testing me to see how far I was going to let this go. I never thought it would go any further, so I had no boundaries or limits. I didn't think I needed any.

The rubbing restarted. He gently massaged my side, my back, and my shoulder. My eyes remained closed. I was present physically, yet mentally, emotionally, and spiritually I had left the room. In fact, I had left the house.

After a few minutes of no rejection on my end, his hand slid under my right arm, near my breast. Chills permeated my body. My eyes had been closed, but when this happened they opened quickly. Why didn't I stop him then?

The room was dark. My niece was asleep at the foot of my bed, in my son's toddler bed. My son was asleep in the room, with his brother, and two male cousins. It was late at night or early in the morning. It was quiet.

His fingers crept toward my breast. Frozen physically, chills flooded my body, again. I remained in a frozen state as I stared at the bedroom door that was shut. His right hand enveloped my right breast and he started massaging it slowly. More chills flooded by entire being. In that moment, he was no longer who he was, to me.

As I mentioned earlier, it has been years since I had been touched by a man. I was heavier than I had ever been. I was recently divorced and felt sincerely undesirable. I was broken and severely damaged.

This was a man I trusted with my entire being. This was a man who I believed loved me. This was a man whom I loved, dearly. His touch was soothing. It was comforting. It was pleasurable. It was wrong.

He gently tugged my body in a way that told me to roll over. Without hesitation, I complied. I was no longer myself.

I was now on my back and he was on my right hand side. My eyes were closed. I didn't know what to expect next and I am not sure I had any expectations at all.

He pulled my shirt up. Then, he dropped his head until his mouth touched my breast. He kissed and sucked on me, slowly and gently.

He kissed and sucked on one breast, as he massaged and played with the other. My eyes were still closed. I was overcome with emotion. Every nerve in my body was now triggered and my senses were heightened. I felt like I was floating in the air.

He kissed on my belly as he slowly insert his hand down my pants. I didn't stop him. Remember, in my mind, when the first clear sexual touch happened, he was no longer who he really was to me and I was no longer myself.

He readjusted himself. He was now straddled over me, but not so much that he couldn't pull my pants down. I had on some baggy, grey, girl seats. They were very loose fitting and easy to pull down. Slowly, he took them off.

I believe he moved so slowly because he was testing me and my approval of his behavior. From the moment his hand touched my breast, he was no longer who he was to me. He became a man who desired me and I needed to be desired.

FLASHBACK - My ex-husband had cheated on me and given me a bacterial infection. That was a breaking point for me in my marriage. Then, a month later, after I had decided to forgive him I caught him on the telephone with a woman. That was the straw that broke the camel's back. I desired my husband. I used to cry and beg him for sex. He'd deny me, yet he was sleeping with other women. Random women, at that.

It wasn't enough that I had waited for him to parole. I was his leading lady for almost three years while he served time in a maximum security prison. We were married while he was locked up. We met while he was locked up, five years prior to getting married.

It was my past experiences with men that led me down a path to become emotionally attached and involved with a convicted felon. My child's father had abandoned me, told me I was not good enough to be his woman and that no other man would ever want me because I was used goods. The boyfriend before him cheated on me while we were apart during the summer. I was a survivor of rape, molestation, and a broken heart on more than one occasion.

Although I never sought fulfilment by becoming promiscuous, when I did get involved in a relationship I was very clingy. I struggled with insecurity. I struggled with trust. I struggled with feeling like I was worthy or enough for any man or boy I was with. I struggled with believing I was desirable.

This man never made me feel unworthy. He was my protector. He was my friend. He was my hero, in a sense. I can remember walking through the grocery store with him, holding onto his arm, with a huge smile on my face as I gazed up at him. I was so proud to be near him. I truly admired and loved him.

Once my pants were down, I remembered I was on my cycle. I grabbed my pants to motion to pull them up as I whispered, "I'm bleeding." I was aware. I was alert. Yet, I was still absent, if that makes sense.

He moved my hands and continued pulling my pants and panties down. He didn't seem to care that I was on my cycle or he didn't hear me. He placed his head in between my legs and it seemed like the room started to spin.

FLASHBACK: I was molested as a little girl. My first sexual experience involved an older female performing oral sex on me. Although I was no older than six years old, I enjoyed what she did. It felt good. I didn't know it was wrong, until we got into trouble after I told on us.

Since that experience receiving oral pleasure has always been a weakness of mine. He knew this because I had shared it with him. I shared it with him because I trusted him. He used my weakness against me.

The warmth from his breath hovered over my clitoris. When his lips touched it, my body shivered, as I threw my head back. It felt good and I went in and out of awareness as he gave me oral pleasure. I was present and I wasn't all at the same time.

I had on a tampon. He didn't care. As he performed oral sex on me, he slowly pulled the tampon out. I didn't even realize this until he climbed on top of me and inserted himself.

In that moment, I blacked out. It was as if I was no longer in my body, but I was. I don't remember how long he was on top of me or exactly how it all ended. I do remember staying quiet knowing that my children and nephews were in the next room and my niece was still asleep at the foot of my bed. When he was done, he climbed off of me as I laid there in the dark. Suddenly, I realized I had just had sex, with my older brother.

We weren't kids. We had kids. We were full grown adults. I was divorced. He was separated from his wife, but he was still married. We were under the influence of alcohol, but we weren't drunk. We knew what we were doing, but neither of us stopped it. Why? How? Sickening, right?

This was more than six years ago and I don't have the answers. I don't have a reason or justification of why I didn't stop him or fight him off. I don't feel guilt, yet I feel extreme shame about what happened.

A counselor told me that since I had been raped and molested before this took place that I did experience black out and I disconnected from reality. I never went back to that counselor and have yet to undergo therapy for what happened. I do know that I don't blame him, I blame us. We both knew better, yet we both allowed what happened to happen.

Yes, I was molested as little girl. I later learned (from another family member) that my older brother was also molested as a little boy. We don't have the same mother, but we have the same father. In our family line there is sexual abuse and addiction. We succumbed to it. Not once, but a few times.

After the first incident, we didn't talk. In fact, we barely looked at one another on the days that would follow. I would go to work, come home, go into my bedroom, drink a bottle of whiskey and fall asleep. I kept a small bottle of whiskey in my purse, just to drink myself to sleep each night. He'd be on the patio smoking, drinking, and listening to music. No words were spoken for days.

One evening I was in the shower. I had drunk my whiskey and was preparing for bed. He came into the bathroom without me knowing. He pulled the shower curtains back and scared me. I covered my body. He laughed and left the bathroom. I went into my bedroom to get dressed and he came in there, too. We had sex, again.

There was no conversation. There was no eye contact. There was no pleasure involved, for me. I never fought him off of me. I never said no. I just let it happen.

I do not recall the details or how many days it had been since the first time. I just knew that what we had gotten caught up in was not right. But I didn't know how to get out of it either.

We were living together. It was me and my children, and him and his children. They had moved in with me. We were both working, yet struggling to make ends meet. I knew he needed my help and I kinda needed his help, as well. There was nowhere for him to go if I put him out. I didn't want my niece and nephews to be homeless. I just didn't know what to do. I also thought it wouldn't have been right or fair to put him out because I had never said no or stopped anything from happening. I was as much to blame as he was. I had no one to talk to about it, either.

I look back and think about the fact that he was the older sibling; he was my big brother and my protector. So why did he even start what he did that night? What made him think it was okay to touch me, to taste me, to penetrate me? His little sister.

Our relationship went downhill from there. Less than two months from the first incident, I gave him notice to vacate my apartment. The property manager was never okay with him being there and had worked with me because he was family. But I didn't want to keep having sex with him and things were only getting worse in the home. I didn't know how to get him out of my home or how to stop what was happening.

For the first time, after a few times, I finally told him no. I finally found my voice. When he climbed on top of me, I fought him off. When he fought to stay on top of me flashbacks from being raped when I was 12 years old came about. I didn't care. I closed my eyes and I attempted to push him off of me. He was pissed that I rejected him and treated me so unkind for the next several days.

Even after this incident I tried to make peace with him by inviting him to a friend's birthday party with me. It was in a neighborhood that I didn't want to go into alone. We went to the party, and then we went to the casino. At the casino we had a few drinks and walked around like nothing had ever happened. We were brother and sister just hanging.

As we left the casino, we entered the parking garage elevator. He pushed me into the corner of the elevator and attempted to kiss me. I tried to push him off of me and kept turning my head. He licked and kissed all over my face, my ears and any part of me he could get to as he laughed. He was tipsy and reeked of alcohol. Finally, the elevator doors opened and I was free to get out. I walked to the car as quickly as I could, but I still had to go home with him.

When we got home, I called a male friend, just to have some sort of distraction. I knew what was next. I knew my brother would be coming into my room at any moment to try to have sex, again. I had already agreed to take what had happened to the grave. I had already agreed to forgive him and myself and to just move on. That wasn't enough for him.

We both struggled with an unhealthy desire for sex. We had shared this desire as brother and sister, in general conversation. But it was in those same conversations where he gathered data about me, my weaknesses, my fantasies, and more. He used it all against me.

He entered my room and I was on the telephone. I told my male friend that my brother had just come into the room. My brother didn't know that I had also confided in my friend what had transpired between us. He motioned to ask who I was on the phone with. I lipped the name to him. He motioned back asking if "he knew." I nodded my head. He stormed out of the room.

My friend ended up being my saving grace. My friend had me pass the telephone to my brother. He wanted to let my brother know that he knew what had been going on and it was not okay. I don't know what was said, but I know my brother looked at me with the eyes of death as he listened to my friend. My brother said nothing in response to whatever was being said on the other end of that call. When I retrieved the phone, my friend said, "You will never have a problem with him, again." And I didn't.

He never tried to have sex with me, again. He never entered my room or the bathroom, again. Within two weeks he had moved out of my apartment and took his children with him. He left my place in shambles, probably on purpose, and he didn't give me any money from his paycheck, as he had previously committed to doing. But he was gone and I was free.

I believe my friend threatened my brother. The strange thing is my friend was in prison when the call took place. He was a well-known gang member from the same faction as my brother. Yes, my brother was a gang member. My friend had a lot of clout and was high ranking in prison and on the streets. Whatever he said worked and here I am six years later with no contact from my brother.

I've wondered had my brother always looked at me with lust in his eyes and his heart. I've wondered if he always plotted and planned to get me. Before anything ever happened he tried to convince me that we were not really related. He told me that his mother told him that my mother had sex with my dad's brother and I may be my uncle's child. I think that was a lie he told himself because he had inappropriate thoughts about me and clearly he had a plan to get me.

On the other hand, I was beside myself. I don't even know the woman who didn't fight back or speak up. I don't even know the woman who allowed what happened to take place.

A part of me never wanted to see my brother for the monster he truly is. No matter what he did, I helped make excuses for him. I defended him. He abused his wife and I made excuses for him. Of course, I supported her leaving him or getting to a safe place, but I still made excuses for his behavior. He'd have drunk spells, cause car accidents, and all sorts of things, yet I never did anything to help hold him accountable.

I used to leave my children with him, alone. The mere thought of him harming them makes me want to commit homicide. He would do questionable things that my child would come home and tell me, but once again I made excuses for him. I downplayed his misbehavior. To me, he could do no wrong. I admired him, remember?

What hurts more than anything is the fact that we were close. We no longer communicate and have not had any mutual communication since he vacated my apartment. Not only did I lose a relationship that I thought to be solid in my life, but my children also lost an uncle. In addition, other family relationships were destroyed.

You probably think I am a disgusting human being. How could a grown woman just lay there or participate, on any level, in having sex with her own brother? How could any part of what he did to me, on any occasion, be pleasurable? I don't have an answer. I am ashamed. I am embarrassed. I know that what happened was wrong. This is one thing in my life that I have no explanation for. Again, I don't even know the woman who possessed me during this period in my life.

What I do know, however, is that I have kept this secret for several years. It has tried to kill me from the inside out. I've gone to therapy for other issues and wanted to talk about this part of my life, but was too ashamed. I kept the secret to protect my brother and probably to protect myself because I still don't understand how I let it happen. I also kept the secret to protect my children, my nieces, and nephews – his children, and the family overall.

This is my first time writing about this. Aside from my male friend I mentioned in this story, only a couple of people know about what happened. It took me a long time to tell them, but each time I told someone it opened the door to my own healing.

Keeping secrets doesn't protect the family. In fact, keeping secrets does the family more harm. Holding onto this secret has affected my life in unexplainable ways. Exposing the secret, in turn, has allowed for true healing.

I have since learned that my brother was molested by his aunts and uncles. I have since learned that what he did to me he also did to our little sister and two of our female cousins, if not others. Had those secrets come out, maybe what happened to me could have been prevented. Maybe he would have gotten the help he needed. Regardless, there will be no more secrets. Not in my family and not on my watch.

"Even the darkest night will end, and the sun will rise."

Journey 4

A Living Nightmare

By the time I was 20 years old, I had already been in two abusive relationships and I was about to enter into another one. He came across as a good guy, had taken me out to play pool at a nearby bar, and had even taken me bowling. There was a rare moment that he wouldn't put a smile on my face...little did I know that it was all just a facade to win me over.

At first he would make comments about my hair (it was cut short, and was just growing past my earlobes). Sometimes he would make rude remarks about my weight (although at the time I only weighed 130 pounds and while I stood at 5'5" I was far from chunky, I was thick in certain areas though). He knew about everything that I had been through, and made it seem like he was so disgusted with what I had been put through. There wasn't a single relationship that I had been in that would be classified as "normal" or healthy. And the abuse that I had already endured was about to seem like child's play.

Within six months of being with him, we had gotten an apartment together and I found out I was pregnant. I wasn't supposed to be able to have children, due to the cervical cancer I had when I was 18 years old. I was so happy that I was pregnant and started buying everything I needed for my baby. He came home one day from work and flipped out on me for spending $100, and this is when the abuse really started. Now mind you, this was out of my paycheck and not a single dime of it was his. We had literally nothing for this baby, and I was going to give my child everything they could possibly need. He started throwing items at me and when that was no longer satisfying to him he started throwing punches. He struck my face a few times and even landed hits to my stomach. When he was finally done, he just sat down on the couch and turned on the TV.

Fast forward some years, we had two boys and two girls. These kids are my world and I would do anything for them, including living a life of misery. The day I left him all the kids were at school. I had a few errands to run, so one of my friends from high school, who I had stayed in contact with, was taking me to my appointments. There was an hour in between my last errand and my therapist appointment, so he took me to lunch, worried, because I hadn't been eating. (I have struggled with eating disorders *Pretty* much my entire life and he had been there for me when I first started with my eating problems).

While we were eating and catching up on our lives, my abuser walked in with one of my daughters who had been sent home from school because she was sick. He made a big scene and said, "Just wait till you get home." Well, I still needed to grab my headphones, so I had my friend drive me to my apartment so I could grab them, then he was going to drop me off at my appointment.

I walked inside, walked straight to my dresser, grabbed my headphones and headed back to the front door. My daughter was sitting on the couch and made a comment about how I was on a date and that "he" had told her that. I turned around to him standing behind me and he confronted me. At that point in time the guy was just a friend and I emphasized that to "him". He didn't believe me and started calling me a whore, pushing me around, and telling me that when I got home I was in for a world of hurt. I walked to the front door and as I opened it with shaking hands, he saw my friend's car outside and immediately grabbed for the bat that was behind the door. He followed me outside, yelling that he would make me pay for making him look like a fool. My friend sped off and got me to my appointment.

The moment my therapist saw me, he hurried me into his office, and immediately called the police. I was shaking, my face was drained of any color, and I was sobbing uncontrollably. The police showed up and told me that I couldn't go home and had me call my sister-in-law. I was then informed after getting the confirmation that I could stay with her and my brother that I couldn't go back for my kids, seeing as he had never laid hands on them and they believed that I was the only target.

I fought for two years to get my kids after that. He would constantly use them as pawns in his game to get whatever he wanted out of me. Even though I had left him, the abuse never stopped. Then, one night as I was getting ready to go back to one of my friend's houses, all hell broke loose.

He was already jealous of this friend of mine, he couldn't stand that I was finally making something of myself, and that he no longer had control over me. I had started standing up to him and so had my kids. He blocked the bedroom door when I had gone in to grab one of the books that I had been reading and stood over me. The look in his eyes and on his face were darker than I had ever seen.

He knocked the book out of my hands, started punching me in my face, and in my head. He grabbed the Xbox that I had left for my boys and smashed it over my head. I fell to the floor, but saw the opening between him and the door. I hurried out of it as fast as I could. When I stood back up, the blood was falling so fast and hard out of my head to the point that I could barely see a thing. I could barely hear anything, over the ringing in my ears and the pounding in my head. I just tried my best to get to my phone, which I did, and I was able to send my brother a quick message, which he replied to immediately.

My sister-in-law was already on her way to my house and as soon as I saw that, I knew I would be okay. I heard something behind me and before I could turn or try to get away he had his arm around my throat and was pinning me to the couch. Everything started going black and I couldn't move, couldn't fight. I must have lost consciousness for a few minutes because the next thing I knew I was being dragged by my ankle towards the kitchen and I could faintly hear my youngest daughter crying and screaming, "You're killing mommy." I heard my youngest son crying and screaming and him telling me that night was the night I would die.

I mustered up whatever strength I could and started kicking out. I must have landed a kick or was at least able to struggle free because there was no longer a hold on my ankle. I couldn't see anything except red and even that was foggy. I could hardly breathe, but I made my way to the front door and made it outside. I heard my sister-in-law yelling my name. Then, I was thrown off of the porch. After feeling like I was flying for a while, my head made contact with the concrete and bounced.

He served one week in county jail and was released on bail. He has been on the run since and has been actively searching for me and my kids with the promise of finishing what he started. I finally have my life back. I'm living somewhere he would never think to look. I have friends who care about me (which was something he would tell me all the time that nobody actually cared about me), strangers who reach out to me for help (once I got my story out there, more people are coming out with theirs); I have custody of all four of my kids (which he never wanted, and I'm finding out he started to abuse them when I left him), and I am slowly getting everything I ever wanted out of life, I am still healing physically and helping my kids heal mentally.

"We don't grow when things are easy. We grow when we face challenges."

Journey 5

Lost in the Dark

I identified with being a victim before I knew what the true meaning of the word was. I lived with the shame knowing that by the age of 15 I had been molested by five people, both men and women. People who I thought loved me, who I thought would look out for me, and be there when I needed them. People who my parents trusted with me. I would soon grow to not trust others and become bitter in knowing that *this* doesn't happen to everyone.

I always wonder *why me*? What made it so easy for these people to treat me like they did and act like nothing ever happened? For the sake of time, I will not recount all five people. I will only shed light on the two that set the foundation of the self-destructive behaviors I created.

I remember a time where I was normal. No worries; no cares, a time where I wasn't scared. I was happy about life and the future. I wanted to be a news anchor and I believed I could do it.

My home as a child was busy. People in, people out, some would stay the night; some would stay a few nights. I wasn't bothered because I liked the company.

He was a man who I thought was my friend. He was a friend of the family. He started out staying one night and then a few nights. At first everything was normal. He played with me, we had family game night, and my parents loved him. They spent a lot of time together.

I liked to watch TV, so at night I would sleep in the living room. This would be the place he slept. Well, at first, I would wake up to my panties down. I was about eight years old and I didn't think much of it. I just pulled my panties up and watched TV until I went back to sleep.

Then, there was one night where I wasn't completely asleep. He grabbed me and pulled me to a standing position. I was daggling like a rag doll. He pulled my panties down and rubbed his penis in my bottom area. I didn't move because I didn't know what to do. I was in shock that this was even happening. I felt paralyzing fear. It was like I had no control of my movements.

When he finished, he laid me back on the couch. I pretended to stay sleep a little while longer. For some strange reason, I didn't want him to know that I had been awake the entire time. I knew what he did to me that time, but all the other times I had no clue what happened. Once I woke up, he told me to pull my panties up. After that everything changed.

My mind raced with so many thoughts. How many times did he do this? What else did he do while I was asleep? Why didn't I just go to the room and sleep? Why would he do this to me?

He told me we were close, like family. Family wouldn't do this to me. At this point my trust began to dwindle.

I woke up a couple nights in the same position - my panties down. He never told me to pull my panties up, again. Why didn't I tell my parents? Well, I was scared. I didn't know how to tell them. I wasn't sure what happened, or how to even explain what was going on. I didn't even know how to start the conversation. *"Hey mom, hey dad, the guy you let spend the night is fondling me while I am sleep. What he is doing I and not quite sure, but he is doing something."* I just didn't know how to say or do it.

Then, there was the fear of a big fight, or a split in our family. How would he react? Would he lie and act like nothing happened? There were too many things to consider and I decided at that moment to just not tell them.

Every day I wanted to tell them. My mom always told me that if someone touched me to tell her. I just couldn't find the right time and place to tell.

After a while, he moved on and I felt better and safe. I saw him around a few times, but I never mentioned it or acted differently around him. I did what I had to do to forget what happened. Until it happened again, with someone else

I was about 13 years old. At first, he would just come and hang out with my parents. Then, he would stay one night and then another. My parents worked the night shift, so this guy became my babysitter.

At first, it was normal; he was very friendly. I learned my lesson from the last time to go in my room to sleep. I thought I was safe in my room. Then, one night I woke up again to my panties down and what sounded like someone running down the hallway. I pulled my panties up and went back to sleep.

I don't know why I didn't notice the signs that this was happening, again. I started to notice what was going on when he approached me during the day. I asked if I could go to the store. He told me, "Yes," and said "When you get back I will teach you how to kiss." I gave him the best *oh hell no* face I could make. Then he said, "No, not on me." In my mind I was thinking, *"On whom then,"* because it was only me and him around.

The night creep-ins to my room happened a few more times. Then, one night I felt pain in my lower area. I woke up immediately as a result of the pain to find him looking out the window. He told me the same dreadful words I heard the other guy say years earlier, "Pull your underwear and pants up."

I started to wear pants to bed thinking this would be some sort of protection. Again, I had no proof; I didn't see anything. How do I tell my parents this? How would they understand? Would I be blamed? I wasn't ready to take that chance so I kept quiet, and did my best to stay away from him.

My parents would send my younger sister to another sitter, but now she was staying at home with me. I couldn't tell them what he was doing, but I could keep him from doing to her what he did to me. So I formulated a plan. During the day, my sister went to daycare, so she was protected. She was always with my mom and dad during the day after daycare, so she was safe there. But at night she wasn't safe. So I would bring her into the room with me and put her in the bed. I would lay on the floor, in front of the door, with it closed. I said to myself that he had to move my lifeless body out of the way to get to her. It is funny how I thought of myself as lifeless. He tried and just as I thought I could feel him pushing the door, he would leave.

After a couple of times he didn't try anymore, but I kept sleeping on that floor. I was determined with everything in me to not let him get to my sister. Eventually he left and we would only see him every once in a while. When I saw him I pretended like nothing happened. But I can't help to think why both of these men thought it was ok to do this. It felt like they had a meeting on how easy prey I was. What was it about me that showed that I wasn't in need of love or protection?

At first I was hurt, and then I became bitter. Then, I became hateful. I hated the fact that I had to be a big girl at such a young age. I hated that I didn't have anyone who had my back. I felt like I was the only one going through this.

From this trauma, I developed a fear of the dark. The dark is where people got the strength to touch me. I figured with the lights on I am protected. The light was my only source of comfort to sleep.

I wondered if I was a virgin. I didn't know what was done to me while I was asleep. I didn't have that open, non-judgmental source of communication with my parents, in regards to sex. Sex was a touchy subject. I asked a few friends, but they were no help. So I felt it was best to keep it in.

I began to hate myself, how I looked, who I was. I felt like I somehow deserved the bad things that happened to me and others deserved better. I became depressed, but back then I didn't know it was depression.

I isolated myself, I cried alone a lot, and I thought about death more than anyone should think about it. I lived not looking for good things to happen. I waited to see what would happen next. My day dreams were filled with all the things that could go wrong in that day. How I could die or end up hurt. I thought I was cursed. Cursed to live a life on continuous bad circumstances.

I only paid attention to the bad because I didn't feel like I was worth more. I didn't feel *Pretty*; I really didn't like me at all. I hid it well. Inside I was dying, but on the outside I was dressed to the nines, with a big smile. I didn't make friends because I knew that I couldn't share this part of me. I also didn't trust anyone, so it's kind of hard to make friends when you have no intention of trusting them with any information, or because you are afraid of what they will do to add to the hurt you already felt.

I was very lonely among people. I felt damaged, used, unworthy, and unloved. I lived in pity for years. Every now and then I would reach out for a lifeline, but would soon feel the reality of their failure to give me what I needed.

I knew God. I went to church, but I was blocked by the lingering question why would someone who loves me so much let so much happen to me? I didn't ask for this life, and I was forced to live the nightmare.

Then, I started to read. It started with self-help books, autobiographies, and the Bible. I saw a pattern. The people I read about dealt with things that they shouldn't have, life altering things, and kept going. I also learned that my source of happiness and joy starts with me. I have the power to change my life, and how I looked at what happened to me.

Since death wasn't an option, I gave life a try. I also sought professional help. I was able to mention for the first time there that I was molested and this helped me see how my future was being affected. Les Brown, a well-known motivational speaker says, "Tell yourself I deserve good things to happen to me, every day. Say it until you believe it." I didn't think I deserved the best life had to offer because of what happened to me. The people that molested me made me think I wasn't worthy of protection.

Getting married, having kids, and having friends were all off limits because I wasn't supposed to have them. Only special people get those types of lives and I wasn't special. With the help of a professional, however, I realized that these were all lies that I repeated out of shame due to what happened to me. Keeping it inside wasn't doing me any good. I was killing myself, slowly.

I didn't even know who I really was at my core. I kept reading, going to church, and developing my relationship with God. He showed me that He was protecting me. All those times I tried to kill myself, He let me live.

Finally, I was able to experience some good things in life. I was able to become a mother and a wife. I have friends that have helped me through my process of healing. I have my days, but day by day it gets easier. I am looking for good things to happen. I smile now and it is genuine. I am not 100% in love with myself, but day by day I find things that I like about me a little bit more.

I am enough, I deserve good things to happen to me, I am beautiful, and I am loved by God. I will continue to say this until it is true in my heart. I think it is time to turn the lights off and face the dark.

"Don't cry to give up, cry to keep going."

Journey 6

A Love that Restores

Living in a world where it screams the word "no" can lead to some places of self-destruction, I have learned through my experiences and the love of Christ how to endure victoriously. Early in life, Satan attempted to take me out of the game because he understood my potential. The problem was I didn't. Rejection was the name he had given me, with a purpose to steal, kill, and destroy all hope for my future.

My parents divorced when I was three years old. Being a mommy's girl, I just wanted to be with my mother. I remember one of the first times I accepted my name. My parents both went their separate ways, and I wanted to go and live with my mother. The answer was, "No;" I was to live with my father. I didn't understand why I could not go with her. Something inside of me began to tell me she didn't want me. As a child, I began to realize what the word *no* meant and later in life realizing what it could do to a person who internalizes it incorrectly. It allows you to believe that no one could genuinely love you and it takes you to places that eventually wipe away your smile. How could the world accept you and love you when the person who birthed you said *no* first?

I grew up with my dad, a family of seven, and I landed smack in the middle. I knew I was different by the way I was treated. I was the only one who wet the bed and everyone's answer to sharing a room with me was *no*. Not even the baby who had her own room was to share it with me. My room was the hallway closet, away from everyone, surrounded by four bedrooms right across from the bathroom. It was a perfect fit for just my bed and the reflection of the toilet.

For me, *no* became a familiar word in our home. We had a washer and dryer in our two-story home, but *no* I was not allowed to use them. My clothes were to be cleaned at the laundromat facility. There were times the family would gather around downstairs to eat, but there was *no* plate prepared for me. My siblings even had a ride to school and back home while passing me by as I walked. I never knew that it was wrong to be treated like that. I didn't even think that it was something I should have discussed with anybody. I never questioned why them and not me. I had already accepted my false identity.

I will never understand how you can grow up with siblings you do not know, to have a baby sister in the same home you were never allowed to hold. I became a lost little girl who had had no voice, being told by my father what to do and how to do it. Whenever I made a mistake, a slap to my face or a punch to the stomach would get me back on track. While girls were dancing with their fathers, I was wrestling with mine. The times when I thought I was actually doing okay, he would whip me anyway, telling me it was preparation for the "just in case." While I would beg him to go places with my friends, my father would laugh as he would ask me did I really want to go. I would become excited for a second, at just the thought of getting away, until he laughed even harder with the answer *no*. He would explain to me how his internal gut told him not to let me do things.

I left home at the age of 16. A new school and a fresh start. A place where no one knew my name or my past. Becoming pregnant at 17 that idea sure did not last. I constantly thought about what others thought of me being so young and expecting. I was already almost four months pregnant when I found out. No time to even think about backing out. The doctor announced it by asking me if I wanted a boy or a girl. I felt like it didn't matter because I wouldn't be a good mother to either. When I brought the news to my family, immediately my mother stopped talking to me and my father laughed hysterically. I remember him telling me that everything I ever did to him would now finally come back to me. I guess that was his prayer for his daughter. A man of God who served his church faithfully.

I gave birth at just 21 weeks. It was June 2, 1998. My peers were making memories at prom and I was left with little time to make big decisions for my family. While giving birth, I had no one in the delivery room to hold my hand and walk me through it. There was no one to cheer me to push or to tell me I could do it. I felt scared and alone as I wondered what I was going to do.

My daughter's father called me once to let me know he would be at the hospital when his daughter arrived. I guess I wasn't good enough for anyone to be at my side. In an instant, my life changed. I was now a mother, but still had school the next day. I had to leave my first child in the incubator weighing only three pounds.

I caught the bus alone, to the hospital, every chance I could, just to see my baby. I worked hard and somehow thought I had it all figured out. Not long after that I realized the things you face when you are young follow you along your path. I ignored raising my child and meeting her needs. To face her, meant I had to face me. My focus was on pursuing her father; even though it was evident he did not want me.

Married at 23 years old, I thought I was saying yes to the love of my life, only to find out I was saying yes to me. I proposed to myself, purchased our wedding rings, and had our home built from the ground up. I did everything by myself and bragged about living the dream. I never thought for once about what Satan was doing to me. He was setting up situations every chance he could to confirm my name. He wanted to make sure rejection would never ever leave me.

While I chose to live in a make-believe fantasy, my husband chose drugs, women, and games. All set out to destroy me. I would laugh at myself for thinking someone could ever pick me. Feelings of rejection have a special way of telling you every single thing that is wrong with you. It taunts you in the night whispering in your ear, *"it will never be your turn to be welcomed and accepted."* You live life without family, or friends, out of fear of getting too close to anyone.

As a young woman, I realized I was hurt and my hurt became my anger. It all slowly transformed me into a pit bull, in which I protected myself out of worry of being hurt, again. I was hurt by the world and angry with myself for not being someone people could want. I didn't know this was all in my head and grooming done by an evil spirit. I didn't understand at the time that nothing was wrong with me and that some people just weren't meant to be a part of my destiny. I fought extra hard to keep people in my life who simply were not supposed to be there.

The fact of losing person after person just broke me. I started to imagine what life would be like without me. I had it all figured out. I would spend one last birthday coming up with my two children. I would then exit out knowing this world would be better off without me. My shame didn't want anyone to know. I came up with the plan to call my now ex-husband, who was engaged to his new bride-to-be, to make him promise to never tell my children. I asked him to make up a lie and tell them I was sick. I had failed in life and didn't want people to see me as a failure in my death. The one last person that could have helped take me off that ledge had in return asked me to come visit him to use me one last time and I went.

I never thought in life I could steep so low. I never wanted to be the woman who would become the mistress to her own husband. Sneaking over to their home, looking at their pictures on the wall and her little I love you notes, internally destroyed me. I found out that this was the same woman who showed up in the picture right before he left me. I remember the time he told me how he got on one knee and proposed to her, in front of her family. The whole time he talked I screamed asking a God I did not know, "WHAT ABOUT ME?!"

Moving forward, I was now a mother of three with a new husband and unexplainable joy knowing that God indeed had a plan for me. I thought my darkest days were over. Eventually, I became worn out in hiding and it was time to face me. A lot of relationships were ruined and deep down inside I still was not happy. I was a child who couldn't forgive her mother and hated being in the presence of her biological father.

There were places I had not been that only God could take me to truly set me free. Darkness lives there and He is the only source of light, a place where there was only one mirror that would show me I would one day shine bright. I was afraid to look at myself in that mirror. I was a wounded woman unrecognizable from what I had allowed the world to do to me. Step by step God unwrapped each bandage that I used to cover my injuries. I never knew someone could love me in this way until the bandages were all gone and He kissed me. He gently came down and looked me right in the face. He told me that He wanted me and if I would just trust Him he would restore everything.

I took a journey that did not include getting back at people based on what they had done to me. My journey actually involved me facing myself and what rejection had done to me. It wasn't about the people, but the way I responded. It wasn't about the lack of love, but the wall that I had built. Brick by brick, we tore that wall down – me and God.

Freedom to me is when you're surrounded by nothing, but the love God intends for you to have. A love that can restore a relationship between a mother and a daughter. Bringing them into harmony and becoming the best of friends. A love that restores a relationship between a father and a child. Where every week they can sit down and share a meal and enjoy each other's company. A love that restores the relationship of and ex-husband and ex-wife, as co-parents. Freedom to be friends and truly love the bonus mother of your children. God has been good to me and through hard work I am finally living my life with the tools that help me every day to genuinely love me.

"I am not free while any woman is unfree,
even when her shackles are very different
from my own."

Journey 7

Unbroken

On Tuesday, May 28, 2019, I went in for an MRI. I am gearing up for spinal surgery to try and mitigate the damage done to my neck. This will be my third surgery. Though my first surgery gave me full use of my legs back, and the second gave me the remainder of my left arm back, my surgeons tell me that there is no fixing it. I will be living with this, and periodically getting surgery to hopefully retain full use of my limbs for the rest of my life.

I am fortunate that I lived through my ordeal, far too many of us don't. Twenty three years ago I was a feisty, determined, pregnant college student. I was a well-established member of the Goth community. I had good, caring, protective friends and a path in life. The father of the child I was carrying had vanished, but I was very well cared for by a close knit group of people.

Through a mutual friend, I met a charming, attractive, young man that was not put off by my being already pregnant. After some time, he decided to step up and assume the role of the baby's father. When I gave him the father bracelet in the delivery room, he cried. I thought I had found a great partner.

It didn't take him long to fall short of the mark, though initially he wasn't abusive, per se. He was just a lazy pain in the backside. He came from a family where abuse was a way of life. His father was gleefully sadistic, and used to physically abuse his mother a great deal. Though he quit drinking and quit beating her after an epic incident, his father still financially, mentally, and emotionally abused his mother. Initially, it seemed he had broken the cycle of abuse. He was rough around the edges, yes. But he wasn't mean, yet. We were really quite happy together, until I doubled my salary with a job switch.

I need whoever may read this to understand that the victims of domestic abuse are not necessarily the people you think. I was not some mousy quiet person afraid to take risks. I was a force to be reckoned with, at work. It was the late 90s, and the tech boom was roaring. I was in the hottest field, in the second hottest market in the world. When I tell you we could write our own tickets back then, I am not kidding. Unfortunately, his ego couldn't take the fact that I made literally double what he did, and so it began.

He became petulant, and passive aggressive. He stopped contributing to household chores completely. He would spend all the money on I still don't even know what, and made the mortgage late, more often than not. When I would confront him, he'd act like it was all my fault. When I would shut off his atm card, he'd cash checks at the bank. When I tried to open another account without his name on it, he had a fit. I was making enough money to support us, but I couldn't because he'd spend it all. It got even worse when he lost his job. Then he had more time to spend money, and zero contribution to it.

It reached a point where I had no choice but to tell him to get a job, or get out. I told him flatly I could afford the house, I could afford my daughter, but I couldn't afford him. He moved back to his parents for a week, and proceeded to get one of the two jobs that would ultimately sabotage my career. He got a job working at a convenience store and quickly got promoted to store manager. That sounds great on paper, but is miserable in real life. For most of the time he worked there he had to open the store at 5 am. I was driving him to work at 4:30 in the morning.

After a few months of this, I convinced him to get a different job because it was killing both of us. So, he got a job working at an upscale department store. Again, sounds great on paper. Except, this time, he took second shift. The car we had, a Saturn, broke down, and he refused to get it fixed. He would constantly insist that we couldn't afford to get it fixed, that it wasn't worth fixing it, etc. I had the privilege of working from home if I didn't need to be at a client site. Because of this, he refused to take the bus, unless I did have to be at a client site. This would drive me to breakdown. Controlling and abusive behavior comes in many, many flavors. Leveraging my own need to please and live up to everyone's expectations of me was his.

My week days would go as such: 6 am I would get up to get my daughter to school by 7:30 am. It was a half an hour away with the legendary DC traffic. 8 am I would get back home and try to do some work while he slept. He had to be to work at 1 pm in Bethesda, Maryland. This was before the Inter-County Connector was built, so that was a 45 minute drive, each way, in traffic. I would get back at about 2 pm. I would eat some lunch and get back on track with work by around 3 pm. My daughter had to be picked up by 5:30. That meant leaving the house by 4:45 pm. I would get back by about 6:30. Dinner, household chores that he refused to do, and taking care of my daughter took the evening. I had to be outside waiting for him to get off at 10 pm on the dot, or he'd start in badgering and criticizing me, calling me a selfish bitch, or a cunt, and not leave it drop for days on end. I'd get home at 10:30 pm, put my daughter to bed, and try to work some more. I slept maybe four hours a night, if I was lucky, for almost a year. It broke me.

During this year of hell, there were multiple incidents of physical abuse. We would fight over him spending all the money, and refusing to do household chores. We would fight over him refusing to take the bus, or get the Saturn fixed. I got so furious and spun up one time. I am ashamed to say I slapped him in the face after he called me a crazy bitch. He proceeded to beat me so badly the right side of my jaw was visibly swollen for a week. I had to go to a client site that way. I covered the bruising with makeup, but I couldn't cover the blood spot in my eye, nor the swollen jaw. He would punch me a few times, and then ask if I was done. If I struggled, or tried to fight back, he'd punch me in the jaw some more.

On one occasion, while the Saturn was broken, and before I got the second car, we had borrowed a friend's car. For some reason, even he wasn't sure of why he decided I needed to return it right then, and tried to force me into the car. I was struggling to get away from him, and he proceeded to shove my face into a mound of compost and dirt we had bought from the town to try to landscape part of the yard. One of the neighbors who happened to be a social worker heard me screaming, and came to investigate. He asked me if I needed help. I was so scared and mortified, I told him no and he left. Thinking back, I guess I kind of understand why he just left. My ex-husband is a very violent and mean person. He was a kick boxing champion. He ran the streets in a gang in his youth. When he wants to menace a person, it is really quite intimidating. I wager our neighbor feared for his own safety.

Over time he manipulated me into believing all these things were my fault. That he was simply having reasonable responses to what I was doing wrong. He had me so convinced I was crazy, and what he was doing was reasonable, I checked myself into a hospital. I tried to bend my mind into his reality. I tried every anti-psychotic on the market, convinced I was completely insane.

One Sunday morning, after a late night of partying, it was well past his turn to get up to greet my daughter when she came home from her grandmother's. He refused, again. I was so tired and frustrated I picked up a mug of water, and threw it at the wall next to the couch where he was asleep with the intention of getting him wet. Much to my horror, it bounced. It hit him.

He flew up from the couch, and came after me. I was begging him, "No, please, I didn't mean for it to hit you." It didn't matter. That cold, mean, menacing look was in his eyes. He beat me down to the living room floor, hitting my head on the coffee table on the way down. As he was wont to do, he stopped hitting me, and asked me if I was done. I said yes, and grabbed a full bottle of Klonopin I took for severe anxiety, and emptied the whole thing into my hand fully intending to kill myself. He hit them out of my hand, snatched me up, put my arms behind my back and my torso down over the arm of the sofa. He then pushed me down so hard that my neck made a sick pop and gave way. He had crushed, and herniated three discs in my neck. I lost 80% of the use of my left arm for eight months, and had weakness until my second surgery 12 years after.

I want to tell you this was the moment that made me leave, but it wasn't. It was the moment that shattered me. I completely submitted, and then went through 14 more years of him. I lost my career, my house, and worst of all, my daughter left to live with her grandmother. He did get less physically abusive, but became a full blown verbally, emotionally, and financially abusive couch-potato alcoholic.

We had a son together in 2002. It wasn't until he went after my kid, jabbing him in the throat, "teaching him to block," that I had enough. Something finally clicked in my head, and the spell he had on me broke. I turned his patient manipulations against him, and over a period of a year, I convinced him he wanted to leave.

After a three-year, vicious, custody battle, I have full legal and physical custody of my son. My daughter is a wonderful grown woman, with emotional scars for which I will always feel guilty. We have a three year, total non-contact, protection from abuse order.

I still have nightmares, but they are getting fewer. My son has opened up, again. My daughter speaks to me, again. I bought another house. The ordeal is finally over, and we are beginning to heal. My dearest wish is that my story may save another person from what we went through.

"A hero is an ordinary individual who finds the strength to persevere and endure in spite of overwhelming obstacles."

Journey 8

Delayed Not Denied

At birth, I was swiftly taken away from my mother. She did not understand at the time what was happening. I was taken to another hospital to receive surgery to try to correct a birth defect that I was born with called Spina Bifida. In Spina Bifida, a developing baby's spinal cord fails to develop properly. Spina Bifida is rare birth defect with fewer than 200,000 U.S. cases per year.

During the time that I was treated for Spina Bifida, I was also treated for a condition called Hydrocephalus. Hydrocephalus is also known as water on the brain. To treat hydrocephalus, a shunt is inserted surgically into the ventricle to drain excess fluid. Shunts are commonly used to treat Hydrocephalus, the swelling of the brain, due to excess buildup of cerebrospinal fluid. If left unchecked, the cerebrospinal fluid can build up leading to an increase in intracranial pressure. This can lead to intracranial hematoma, cerebral edema, crushed brain tissue or herniation. The cerebral shunt can be used to alleviate or prevent these problems in patients who suffer from Hydrocephalus or other related diseases.

My mother was a teenager. She had her own health issues. It was determined that it would be in my best interest to be placed for adoption. My birth mom found it tough to give me up, but if I was to have a fair chance at a normal life, she had to let me go.

As an infant, I went into a foster home, where I stayed until I was placed with my adoptive family. In 1981, when I was two years old, I was placed and my name was changed. They called me Missy so that I didn't lose my identity completely.

Although I now had a family to love and care for me, there were some rough times. I started walking late due to my condition. I suffered from pains in my spine that went unexplained. These pains were so intense, that I would fall to the floor suddenly. My parents took me to different doctors trying to figure out what the issues were, but they would always leave empty handed and feeling defeated.

God showed me favor at a very early age. See, there are so many people with this same condition who are unable to walk. I learned to do what the doctors said was impossible. I was determined to walk.

My parents thought it was funny watching me pull myself up by holding onto the table leg and refrigerator door. My parents believed that all things are possible with God, so they decided to take me to see an Evangelist who "laid hands" on me. It's unknown when I started walking, but once I started, I couldn't be stopped.

I stayed in plenty of daycares. Each experience was bad. I had a fear of darkness and the teachers either didn't understand or didn't care.

My mother has literally flipped out on a teacher for sitting on me. I started staying with a sitter at her home. This lady had a maid who took care of the children. Babies were upstairs and the big kids were in the basement.

There was never anything for us to do in the basement, so some of the kids came up with the idea of inventing our own fun. Some of the girls who knew where the linen closet was thought it would be a good idea to use sheets as a jump rope. The basement light was busted out because of this and we all got in trouble. We didn't get time out, we got beaten. Even the ones who didn't participate got beaten, as well. I remember getting beat so bad that I had welts on my legs and back. My parents took me to the hospital and they told them to take me out of her home or they could lose me.

I was more than happy to leave because this sitter would force me to eat things I wouldn't normally eat. I spent a lot of time in my aunt's home with her family. This is where I would be until I started school. I was comfortable in her home. Her three children were older than me, but they felt more like older siblings. I use to wonder why she wasn't the one to adopt me.

At the age of 15 years old I became pregnant. This came as a shock, not only because of my age, but because all my life I was told I would never be able to have children because of my birth defect. I remember the day I found out, I was laying in the floor because I was hot. I had the ceiling fan on and a window up and I still couldn't seem to cool off. My mother brought home a pregnancy test the next morning for me to take.

With a positive test in front of me, I was still in denial. I went to the doctor where they confirmed that I was indeed pregnant. The nurse spoke to me about my options and what would be best for me. She spoke of adoption and abortion. Neither was an option for me. I was going to have my baby and do right by him or her.

I think people wanted me to be ashamed or embarrassed and I was neither. I knew this was my gift from

God and I knew he wouldn't allow anything that I couldn't handle to come my way. I remember telling his father that I was pregnant and he said those famous lines most guys use, "It's not mine!" I wasn't going to beg him to beg him to be in our child's life, so I stopped seeing him for a while.

The first trimester was rough! I was sick every day so I didn't gain much weight in the beginning. By my third trimester I started dealing with depression. I thought that I wouldn't make it through labor and delivery. I shut myself off from people out of fear of what I thought was about to happen to me.

All of my doctor's appointments were just my mother and I. She was there for everything. By the end of my pregnancy I weighed 200 pounds. Sleep was nearly impossible.

On February 14, 1995, I went into labor. My mom called my dad at work and he got off to take me to the hospital. I arrived to labor and delivery around 3:30 in the afternoon.

My mom called my son's father on his job so that he would come to see his son being born. He didn't come. He said he couldn't get off work to come.

I received medicine for pain immediately. The medicine worked a little too well because I couldn't feel anything and they wanted me to be able to feel when I needed to push. They ended up reducing my pain medicine and at that point I could feel everything.

At 8:06 pm, Tuesday night, I gave birth to a bouncing baby boy weighing 6 pounds, 14.2 ounces. My mom's sister was by my side during the time I was pushing. She helped to keep me together. Even at my age, I was a proud mom. My son was my heart in human form

I've searched high and low for love and never knew what it was until I had my son. I still desired something more. There had always been something missing from my life.

Growing up, I never heard I love you so I went searching for it. I wanted it so bad that I believed almost anybody that said it to me and it wasn't until they showed me different, that I would believe anything else. I became really cold hearted and I didn't believe anybody that came trying to show me love. I believed that because I had a disability and that fact that I walked different that I wasn't supposed to feel love. I thank God that He showed me what the other side of pain looked like.

My grandmother had a caregiver that would come take care of her and on weekends her three sons would come with her. Her oldest son was my first crush after the R&B singer Bobby Brown. I was seven years old; he was 12 years old and not thinking about me. I remember sitting next to him on my grandmother's couch and telling him that we would get married someday.

Fast forward to 1998, this same guy came into the restaurant I was working at. I spoke to him and asked him if he remembered me and he wasn't really sure. We chatted for a bit and he showed me a picture of his daughter and I showed him a picture of my son. We exchanged numbers and started hanging out. I was still looking for a love my son couldn't provide.

Things didn't go well with my son's father, so I was single. This young man was also in a situation that he was certain wouldn't last. We officially started dating November 26, 1998.

We had to endure a lot of issues from people who were against us being together. We both knew what we desired and went after it. On weekends when my son would leave to go with her father, we would always get together and hang out. On September 11, 2001, we had breakfast together and we were watching television as the airplanes were crashing into the twin towers. He began to tell me how life is too short to be unhappy and that we both deserved to be happy. He asked me to marry him and we were married on March 16, 2002.

We didn't have our own place yet, so we decided to stay with his mom. Because I didn't know how this would play out, I left my son with my parents. I felt like he would be better off with them. In the beginning, our marriage was filled with a lot of hurt. There was physical, verbal, and mental abuse in the home that I didn't want either of our children to witness. I didn't see him as much as I wanted and that is something that still bothers me until this day.

In 2005, my father took ill and passed away on February 9th. My husband and I moved back in with my mom and son. That lasted all of six months for me because we couldn't get along. I left my son with my mom, again, so she wouldn't be alone and then she suffered a stroke. I took my son with me because I didn't want him to be there and not know what to do if something were to happen. While living with me, my son saw a lot and we've gone through a lot together.

During his senior year of high school, his dad purchased a house and he decided to go live with him. It hurt my feelings, but I never tried to keep him away from his father. My son has always been my world. We grew up together and watching him turn into the man he is today has been amazing. I'm beyond proud of him.

When I got married, I became a step mom, and that little girl showed me that I could love a child I didn't give birth to. She was three when her dad and I got married, so I've been able to watch her grow, heal her through heart break and so much more. I see so much potential in her and I push her to see it in herself. Being in her life wasn't an easy task, but she's been worth every ounce of blood, sweat, and tears I endured to be in her life. Her future is so bright. Her relationship with my son is unmatched. They've been in each other's lives for so long that they look alike now.

There were moments in my marriage where we allowed the enemy to creep in. We've talked about divorce many times. But as much as it was discussed, we fought harder for our marriage. Infidelity tried to consume us as well. We worked through everything designed to destroy a marriage. We wanted to be a testimony for those who may have gone through or are going through the things we had to fight through to get to this place of forgiveness.

Now that the children are older, we don't do family things like I'd like for us to, but hopefully we can work on it. I miss the four of us spending time together like we used to, so we definitely have to try and find that reconnect.

I joined the social site Facebook in 2008 believing I'd be able to locate my biological family. I met people from everywhere, and some have touched my life tremendously. I did a search of my mother's last name not knowing whether or not she was on there or if she had a name change that I was unaware of. I stumbled across two ladies that I felt like I had similar features with. I sent them both messages explaining who I was and what I wanted.

One of the ladies responded and she said my story matched that of her sister. She said she would get back with me because her sister was in the hospital. Before she got back to me, I received a phone call from a number I didn't recognize. It was on March 3, 2010 and I was hearing my brother's voice for the first time since I was placed for adoption.

I remember trying not to cry while talking to him. That day changed everything for me. Most of this was very overwhelming to me. My brother's aunt sent a message and encouraged me to do things my way; to take my time and if it didn't feel right, to handle it accordingly. Over the next few days, I got another phone call. This time it was from a lady calling me by my birth name. I knew without a doubt that this was my mother.

I met her in person, finally. Shortly after, her health started declining and I tried to spend as much time with her as I possibly could. She told me she was getting tired and I wasn't sure what she meant so I suggested she take a nap. Looking back, I think she was telling me her soul was tired. She got sick in January of 2014. My mother always spoke what was on her mind and she didn't care who agreed or disagreed. So, when I was told she was talking out of her head, I didn't know just how bad it would get.

I spent my birthday with her and I told her I'd come back after my son's birthday. By this time, she was taking a turn for the worse. My brother told me they wanted to put her in hospice. To be honest, I had no clue what type of place it was. I told him if that meant she would get better, I was all for it.

There was snow here so we couldn't travel until it melted a little. When we did get there, she didn't look right to me, but I didn't ask any questions. Everyone seemed to know something, but me. I expressed to my aunt that I never got any alone time with my mother and she politely asked everyone to leave the room for a moment. I rubbed her hands and told her I loved her and I'd be there whenever she decided to open her eyes. Later that night, she started to mumble and I looked to my aunt for the ok to say something to her. She shook her head no.

She started asking for her uncle. I decided to get up and I held her hand. I told her I loved her and I honestly believe she said it back. I never saw them try to feed her anything and I wanted to know why.

My aunt explained to me, but her explanation just wasn't working for me. I went and asked someone who worked there why she hadn't had food. I spoke with a Chaplin and he explained to me that she was near death and he felt like because of her condition, she was ready to go home. He told me he felt like I was holding her here and I needed to let go. Of course, I thought this guy was nuts. I called my husband to tell him I was going to stay another night and I told him what was said. Just as I was saying this my husband, my aunt and the Chaplin were slowly approaching me and I knew then something was wrong.

The Chaplin said, "I'm sorry." I moved past him, went into her room and just like that, she was gone. I laid on her chest crying and begging her not to leave me, but she was already gone.

Three years and eleven months was all we had. I keep hearing how grateful I should be because a lot of people don't find their family and I did. They said she could've already been gone, but God gave us time. I am grateful, but I can't help but think of the 31 years we spent apart. It just doesn't seem fair.

I have been trying to figure out who I am for as long as I can remember. I never felt like I belonged in my adoptive family. I've had family members make sexual advances towards me in both families but mainly my adoptive family. Being family doesn't mean much to some especially if someone blood related to you can sexualize you.

I question my purpose in life. Friends and some family said I should share my story that it may help someone who may be in a similar situation. My health has not always been great and as I've aged, I have seen it go from good to bad in the blink of an eye.

Depression and anxiety have gotten the best of me at times. I live my life feeling like I'm in this world alone. I know I have people around me that care, but the ones I feel like should care, don't. There's so much I'd like to learn more about my biological family, but since my mother's death, I don't spend time with them and I don't ask questions.

I feel like God allowed me to meet my biological family to show me why I had to go through what I went through. I met my maternal side of the family, first, then my father's side. I've spent so much time trying to fit in when I was born to stand out. I've come to the conclusion that not everyone loves in the same way that I do and I have to learn to be ok with it. I have my own family now and they come first. I'm surrounded by good friends who are more like siblings to me. I honestly have nothing to complain about. Everything that was designed to kill me, made me who I am today.

"The strongest people aren't always the people who win, but the people who don't give up when they lose."

Journey 9

The Voiceless Child of Adultery

This is for you ladies who feel a piece of a man is better than nothing. It is my prayer that a child will never manifest in your womb, as long as you are sleeping with a married man. It is my desire to help you discover your worth. You are WORTHY! (Hebrews 13:4)

Who am I? I am a child conceived through adultery. I am a child who did not understand my worth. I was born under the demonic spirit of adultery, a spirit that would rear its ugly head throughout my childhood and my adult life. (Proverbs 31:25)

Week One. Dad picks me and mom up from the hospital; it's time to go home, but not before stopping by the local jewelry store. He buys mom an engagement ring and promises to leave his wife. This was the first lie ever spoken over my life. Imagine this, ladies, one week old and being introduced to THE SPIRIT OF MANIPULATION. (Leviticus 25:17)

Elementary School. I was forced to spend time at dad's house, with the women he never left, as promised, for my mother. Whenever his wife looked at me, she was reminded of the pain her husband, my dad, caused her. I'm the spitting image of my mother.

Dad went out at night to feed his gambling addiction, leaving me with a woman scorned. This is where I learned to mask my pain and silence my voice. I BECAME A FATHERLESS AND MOTHERLESS CHILD, at the age of eight years old. THE SPIRIT OF ABANDONMENT (1 Thessalonians 5:24)

Jr. High School. I'm no longer forced to visit dad. I'm old enough to stay home, alone, if needed. Dad would stop by on weekends after meeting the needs of his primary family. This is where I would meet THE SPIRIT OF REJECTION. (1 Peter 2:4)

High School. This is the time mom became the victim of her choices. It was now my job to call dad for money. This is also the time I started resenting my parents. I'M NOT WORTHY, I GET WHAT'S LEFT. THE SPIRIT OF DECEPTION. (Ephesians 5:6)

College. For sure I would receive a free education, after all dad served in the armed forces. Say what? Your wife said no?! You have to respect her?! What is my mom doing? Is she at home? What does my mom have to do with my education? This was the evening my mother gave me the real meaning of NO HONEY, NO MONEY. Later on, the same evening, my father gave me the real meaning of A WOMAN NEVER HAS TO BE BROKE. (Joshua 1:9)

There are several other spirits that falls under the spirit of adultery. For a woman to believe a night of passion will not affect her child/children, she is wrong. It took me years to recover from the emotional abuse I endured, as a result of my mother's choice to lay and have a child with someone else's husband. I struggled with speaking up and sharing my pain when others hurt me. It was easier for me to isolate myself than to speak my truth, because this is what I learned as a child. (2 Timothy 2:15, Ephesians 6:14)

My Healing. I am the voice of the child conceived with a married man. In order for me to heal, I had to understand and believe anything that happened during my childhood was not my fault. The grown people in my life had failed me as a child. How was this possible? I had been protective of my mom my entire life. How could I dishonor her, now? Facing my truth would leave me feeling alone and abandoned, just like that eight–year-old little girl.

Time for Church. Who's going to cast out these demons? I know how to pray, but casting out demons was a whole new level of Christianity. Yes, I have a personal relationship with our Lord and Savior. I was baptized at the age of 16. However, my personal relationship with Jesus started when I was eight-years-old, sitting on stairs, feeling abandoned. My aunt taught me how to pray. She also told me if I was ever afraid just repeatedly shout the name of Jesus as loud as possible; most people respected or feared the name of Jesus.

One thing I have always known is that Jesus loves me. As an adult, I had to stop blaming my childhood for my adult behavior. I had to admit I did not love myself; I was my own worst enemy. I had become the Master Manipulator and the Master of Deception, in my own life. I knew how to make me look fabulous on the outside, but inside I was silently suffering.

The path I chose was so ugly; I was bathing daily in conditional love. A product of the first lie spoken over my life. Every relationship was conditional, including my marriage and motherhood. Why? Because I expected them to protect me from the world I created. Needless to say, they failed miserably. It wasn't their job to protect the little girl living within me. I needed God, Jesus, The Holy Spirit, and a circle of sisters who know and love the Lord.

Sis, I challenge you to start intentionally loving yourself. You deserve better than to lay with a married man and so does your child/children. Walk in God's grace and mercy. It's ours; He's just waiting on you to surrender. Get naked with God, confess your sins.

To the unmarried women, the Bible says, he who finds a good wife finds what is good and receives favor from the Lord. (Proverbs 18:22) It's time you allow that good single man to FIND YOU! Focus on yourself and Jesus and I promise you that man will show up when you least expect him. He will be equipped to love you the way God intended you to be loved.

Get in a Bible based church. Join a small group, you need women who will encourage, inspire, and uplift you along your journey. These are things that helped me so I am sharing in hopes of helping you. You cannot heal without Jesus and a support system of sisters who will hold you accountable, in a loving manner and share their stories with you.

Baptized in The Holy Spirit. I'm a woman of God on a mission to help women live their best life. I no longer subscribe to anything conditional. I stopped listening to lies and abusing myself. I learned how to love me as Jesus sees me. My pain turned into purpose.

I'm on a journey to help women discover their worth. Once you know your worth, you can live your best life. I am my sister's keeper. The joy in my heart is something God gave me when I started fully relying on Him and only Him. I hope me sharing a tad bit of my story will allow you to look at your life from a different point of view. Sis, you can do it! I'm praying for you!

"You will find it necessary to let things go, simply for the reason that they are too heavy."

Journey 10

A Deprived Heir

As a young girl, growing up my mother took great care of me. I am grateful to say I didn't go without having the essentials I needed to survive and I even had the things I wanted. My mom did her best, overall, to raise me and I often wondered how she was able to take care of me. When I observed other families, I felt like we were different from them because there was something missing.

When I was five years old, I tried to figure out this one particular thing, but because I was young I couldn't see through what was going on around me. Not to mention, it was just my mother, sister, and I. My mom was very overprotective of me and because of that I really wasn't allowed to stay at anyone else's house and if I did it was just a couple of people.

When I went to the home of close friends of the family, I noticed how they seemed to have a complete family. I was missing the cornerstone, which was my father figure, in the home. I always wanted to have my father, as a little girl. I must say any man can be a father, but I wanted my dad in my life. I am grateful to say that I didn't act out because I was missing the cornerstone in my home, but there is nothing like getting nurturing from your dad.

As I matured, I realized I had the best DAD a person could ever long for and that is my HEAVENLY FATHER. Once again, my mom did her best raising me in the fear of the Lord and I will not take that away from her. Everything I did, I did with my mom from birth to at least 12 years of age.

At the age of 12, I unknowingly met my biological father. He came to our home in Cedar Hill, Texas with some portraits. I tried to figure out WHY he was in our house, with these portraits. My mom and this man were in the living room looking back and forth at me and these portraits. A couple of days later, my mom mentioned to me that the man in the living room was my biological dad.

Now, imagine growing up in your early childhood and pre-teen years without a dad in your life and then your mom marries someone who is supposed to love and cherish her. Then, surprisingly, this new man that comes into my life that was supposed to take me in as his daughter sexually abused me. Just imagine that! No real father in the home for 12 years, then someone comes along and takes my childhood away. But GOD!

I even carried a last name that was not even my last name. When the teacher called my name on the classroom roster, I had to say "here" to a name that wasn't mine. I was too excited when my last name changed when I got married. The truth of the matter, however, is that in the first eight years of my marriage, I didn't have respect for my husband, nor did I know how to treat my husband, which is very important.

When my husband and I were engaged, I thought I was ready to treat him as "my Lord," however; I hate to say that I failed him as a wife, in the beginning. It took about eight years to realize I wasn't properly treating him as I should have been or how he deserved to have been treated. I often wondered if I had had my dad in the home, would I have learned how to treat a man, especially according to the Bible?!

I never really understood why I was without my biological dad for the first 12 years of my life. When I thought I was blessed with someone who came along to be a dad to me, that man ended up molesting me. There were plenty of days where I blamed God and my own mother for not having my biological dad in my life, since birth. I have often said to myself how could this possibly be the plan and will of God.

Between the ages of 12 to 20 were some of the roughest times in my life. I had to live day by day without having that special person I always wanted to have growing up. I expressed to my husband in the early part of my marriage how frustrating it was to me and he would always remind me how God has been my Father throughout those years. I never really recognized that on my own. I am so grateful how my husband nurtured me through the pain of not having my dad and helped me press through the pain from the days I dwelled in the same home of a child molester.

I want to remind you, again; I didn't see the purpose in me being molested and I never knew it would serve a purpose today. People around me encouraged me and even expressed to me how my going through would help bring the next person through, but I just didn't understand it to be so true. I see now what I went through didn't kill me and how it only made me stronger.

I learned how to look at the positive, even though I went through. I decided to make sure my children didn't go through what I went through. I love to see every day how my own children have their dad by their side and they have been blessed to have their father in their life since birth. Even though I didn't have my biological dad and I had to learn how to treat my husband; I am thrilled to share how the Lord helped me and showed me how to turn my marriage around for the better. All along the answers were in His word.

I will admit these trials I been through have brought me closer to Him and I can testify and say it was only HIM. I survived and my marriage is thriving and growing today. What I went through as a young woman helped determine who I would be today. I want my readers to know that when you are going through difficult times you don't have to settle for what it looks like, even if it seems like it can't be turned around. I want you to believe that you can see outside of your situation and how you will be able to look back and see how God can use the bad things in your life to accomplish His purposes in your life.

I had to realize that if no one ever went through anything how could we help someone who is going through. I see how my trial didn't last forever and something good has even came out of my trial. For one, I have been given a suitable chance to implement tools like faith, forgiveness, and even patience. The most beautiful part of my trial is that since I have been writing, I have become relatable to my audience as I have coached, helped and even inspired others to share their testimonies because of their trials.

I really like Romans 8:28 because my trials did have a divine purpose and I know there is more to come. Everything we face is designed to help us reach the goal that Christ has for us. I have also witnessed how Christ has been good to me even through my trials and for that I am and will forever be grateful.

The only one thing I hate is how I let my trials affect me and what I mean is I produced some bad fruit while I went through my trial and that was not what Christ had for me. I did do things that weren't pleasing to God and I felt I did things because it was just a simple way to relieve stress. I want us all to understand we don't have to turn to sex, marijuana and alcohol when we are going through. However, we should choose Christ over these few things when we are going through. Yes, I will say it is easy to go to those things and use marijuana, sex, and alcohol to cope. However, God is the One to help us gain the freedom and healing that we need. When those unclean things come to mind, we should reflect on James 4:7 and reroute our attention to Philippians 4:8. I had this counsel in my late teen years; however I did what I wanted to do at that time.

I am glad that the Lord has given me more time to get myself together and I am still striving for perfection. All that I have been through was for God's glory and if He can do it for me; he most certainly will do the same for those who feel stuck around me. I am still amazed of what God has brought me from and how the bad has been turned around for my good. I used to think I wasn't growing in my dark places, but God was just building me for my future. Now I am at a point where I want to simply give back to HIM and the only way I can do that is through my worship and the choices I make on a day to day basis.

At my assembly, when we are worshipping, I now try my best to stand up during praise and worship in spite of how I feel. When I sit and think about how God has delivered me due to his reckless love for me, I should always stand without any promptings. I think I gave the enemy too much power in my life and I am here to declare I am here for it! I wish I could have changed some things that occurred, but if that was so, I wouldn't have a story to tell today.

Yes, I was molested as a young girl and stayed in the same home for seven years after that; even though I felt alone, God was with me I didn't see the purpose in why I went through those trials but I now see it was to mature me. I want to remind my readers to be careful not to be so quick to beg God out of situations because we could very well be missing out on the many blessings He has for us. But instead ask God for wisdom while we are going through our circumstances. I wish I would have been more laser focused on Psalm 9:10 and how the Lord said, "He has never forsaken those who seek HIM."

"It's not whether you get knocked down; it's whether you get up, again."

Journey 11

Me, Myself & I

When asked to share my story, I wondered if I would really be able to put down on paper exactly what my life has been like. I felt like no one would really care what I went through or be interested in reading my story. It has been a very rough road and there are some things that no one knows I went through and probably never will. So I guess I will start with a little background information.

My maternal grandmother had 17 children. All were born at home except for the last one. Not sure why I always tell everyone that except to illustrate that they were a very poor, backwoods type of family. My bio mom was one of 10 daughters and seven sons. This was a very large, dysfunctional family.

I was born to her, a young, unwed woman, who already had two children, one that was three to four years old and the other who was 18 months old. What I know about my birth is surrounded by secrecy and death. My bio mom died when she was 46 to cancer; I was 23, so I have many unanswered questions that everyone else in the family believes are not important or just refuses to talk about. They are important to me because it's about who I am, where I came from, and why I was the one that was given away.

I do understand, somewhat, being her third child, she had too much on her plate and she gave me to her sister. I don't know if it was supposed to be permanent or temporary, but while I was there I was told that my bio mom went to her brother and his wife and asked them if they wanted me. They were unable to have children of their own. They told her that they would take me, but under the condition that she never try to take me back.

So, one cold and very snowy day, they set out to drive five hours to my aunt's. I was six weeks old. When they arrived they found me in a back room, in a crib, alone, with nothing on but a thin t-shirt and a wet diaper. I was in *Pretty* dire conditions, malnourished, and not thriving. They took me home and nursed me and loved me as their own. They are my mom and dad.

As I grew up, cousins would tell me I was adopted, but my mom always said that wasn't true and I had my suspicions, but I believed it. When I was fourteen, everything came to a head. After a drunken evening, my dad had accused me of ignoring my cousin because I was on the phone. When I said no, she is sick and ok he slapped me for back talking him. I was hysterical, I ran in my room, locked the door, and climbed out the window and got into my grandmother's (my adoptive mom's mother) car. She ended up taking me to the emergency room.

While there the police showed up (I assume the hospital called them).During their questioning of me I blurted out that my dad had tried to rape my sister. That set off a series of events that involved investigators, child services workers, police, courts, etc. He didn't really try to rape her, but in my hysteria that is how it came out. He had actually fondled her as well as, it turns out, several of my other cousins and who knows where that could have led.

My mom didn't believe me and that crushed me. She accused me of lying and I ended up living with my grandmother for a while. Eventually my dad took a plea that said he wasn't guilty, but there was enough evidence to prosecute him for the molesting or inappropriately touching several of my female cousins, as well as my younger sister. My mom finally admitted that she believed he had done it, but she still loved him and was staying with him.

My bio mom appeared around this time and actually went to court and tried to get custody of me. The judge told her since she hadn't raised me up to this point that she had no bearing in the case. He ruled that my grandmother (the mother of the woman who raised me, so technically my aunt's mother) would have legal custody of me and my mom (my aunt) would have physical custody.

After a lot of work on our relationship I was able to return home. My dad and mom were still together although not for long. It was a very awkward and trying time for a 14-year-old, not to mention dealing with all of this. Not long after I was back home, my mom found out he had been cheating once again and left him. We lived together until I was seventeen, at which time she took him back, again. With a family background like that my self-esteem, confidence, and ability to live with dysfunction was born.

I met my first husband when I was 15-years-old. He was a friend of a friend and 19 years old. He was in the military and we saw each other on the weekends; First, sneaking around, then, with parental permission and lots of rules. We were sweethearts and I thought I knew everything. He was older and experienced, and I was old beyond my years. We got engaged when I was 16 and planned a December wedding, after my 18th birthday.

He got out of the military in May and we discussed how living separately for six months before the wedding was expensive. We moved the wedding up to June. My grandmother had to sign for me to get married because she was my legal guardian. Everyone thought I was pregnant, but I wasn't, we just wanted to be together. Looking back, now I believe that I just wanted to get out of my home, too. My parents' reconciliation was more than I could take and I was tired of the turmoil.

Everything went well for the first year. By the second year, we were filing for divorce. I had cheated on him with a coworker. We had purchased a house that was a half hour away from everything and everyone I knew and he was working shift work. I was alone, a lot. I know it's no excuse, but after growing up in the family I had and seeing everything I saw, it didn't seem unusual to me. Just something that happens.

We were a couple of months from finalizing our divorce and saw each other at a party at a friends' house. We talked and decided that we would reconcile and start over. About two months later, I became pregnant with our first child. She was born when I was 20-years-old.

My first memory of him hitting me was when I was six months pregnant with her. After a misunderstanding on my part, I had thrown a set of keys at him and they struck him in the face. So that evening when I came home we argued and he slapped me. I went flying back on the bed. I should have left then, but I didn't. Where would a pregnant 20-year-old go? I had no money and the original argument was my fault. So I sucked it up.

When our daughter was six months old, I became pregnant with our second daughter. She was born when I was 21. Life was busy then and he went on with working a full time and part time job. I was left with the kids and the house. The weekends were his to do what he wanted.

I felt overwhelmed and alone in this world. My sister was pregnant at the time and I thought, hey, maybe (another) baby would fix everything, (I know…I know, but remember I was only 22-years-old at that time). So baby three, our only son, was born when I was 23.

The Christmas after he was born, was the second time I can recall he hit me. It was Christmas Eve and we needed to put the girls Christmas presents together, but he wanted to go next door to the neighbors and party. I asked him to please help me and then he could go back over to the neighbor's. He was mad, but came over anyway and we were on the kitchen floor assembling their presents. I can't even remember what was being said, but before I could blink he slapped me back across the kitchen floor. I was crying and he didn't care. He finished and went back next door.

By the time our son was six months old, I had another affair. I was craving some affection and attention and this guy was there. He love bombed me and I was blinded by everything. I confessed to my husband and he took it hard. He went out looking for the guy to hurt him or scare him or both and when he couldn't find him, he came home to me. Round three. He choked me up against the kitchen counter and then drug me by my hair down the hallway all while our babies were asleep. Looking back, I believe I had post-partum depression and it fueled my need to find someone to love me and give me the attention I was lacking. I also believe we never fixed our original problems before our first baby was born so they festered under the surface until they couldn't anymore.

Enter husband number two. He was an old high school friend of ours, fresh out of the military with a messed up childhood, too. I thought he was my soul mate. He was so down and alone and when he came around he paid attention to me and the babies. I thought he needed me. I thought I could fix him.

His first marriage was over. He told me how she did him wrong and took his sons and he didn't know where they were. We began dating and during this time I became a full blown domestic violence victim. I should have seen the signs: the drinking, the fighting, trouble with the law, the dui's, etc. I ended up pregnant when my youngest was only nine months old. I was going through my divorce and thought I could handle another baby. He said I had to have an abortion. I didn't want that. My mother, who was totally against abortions, encouraged me to have one, too.

They all thought my ex-husband would take custody of my three babies if he found out I was pregnant. In my mental fog of low self-esteem, depression, and just lack of confidence, I allowed myself to be convinced this was best for everyone around. I told him he had to pay for it. He got angry, but ended up giving me the money. Before my appointment day, he called me and told me to reschedule because he needed some of the money back to pay his rent. So that's what I did. I was under some kind of spell that I couldn't explain to anyone. I had no spirit. I was a shell of who I thought I was.

I got the abortion a couple of weeks later and to this day I will never forgive myself for that. That was probably the worst thing I have ever done in my life. The night I came home after it was over, he was supposed to be helping me with the kids, and he got mad when I asked him to do something. He said I could get up off my ass because I didn't do anything all day and I could do it since he was tired and worked all day. So you think after all that I would have seen the light and left….nope.

We moved in together and that is when everything went to hell. We went out to a club; he drove home and decided he was hungry so he wanted to go to a restaurant. He drove right into a road block. He was screaming at me to trade places with him so he wouldn't go to jail. He said that it would be my fault he was getting locked up and getting another DUI. This began our pattern.

I was the chauffer. I had to get up at 4 am and drag my babies out of bed to drive him to work, and then pick him up. There were days when our heater broke in my car and he wouldn't fix it. I had my children bundled up so much. I felt like a complete failure as a girlfriend and a mother.

Nothing I did was good enough. He was terrible with money and had me keep it when he got paid, pay his bills, and dole it out when he wanted it. He would get drunk and demand it all and when I refused he would break everything I owned: Tables, dressers, knick-knacks, pictures, anything he could get his hands on. I would give him the money and he would leave to go and get drunk.

I have so many memories of the things he put me through. Being at a party and walking into a pop up camper, seeing him doing lines on the table, getting mad, leaving and him following me to the car and choking me on the hood of the car. Nobody noticed or if they did they didn't say anything to him. I felt like this was my life. He cheated on me with his best friend's younger sister and others I couldn't ever prove entirely. But most of all the lies, he was a master at lying to me. I would always find out the truth though.

I somehow managed to finish night school. I went back to work and was able to move us out of assisted living into a decent townhome. It was during this time that I helped him find his sons and we went to visit them in Hawaii, using my tax refund, no less. While in Hawaii, his ex-wife, who is to this day one of my best friends and biggest supporter, told me how their life really was. The alcoholic rages, the beatings, all the things I was living, but couldn't admit to anyone.

I had a miscarriage on the flight home from that visit. Three months later we were married and our son was conceived. Now, I was really in deep. He didn't beat me while I was pregnant, but he did enough verbal abuse, drinking, and getting in trouble with the law during this time.

Our son was born and we bought a house. I know, crazy, but that's how it works. You are in a delusional state that your reality is settling for things that other people would be appalled at. By now we had been together a total of three years. For the next 11 ½ years I lived my life taking care of my children and trying to shield them from all the abuse that I was receiving.

I felt like a single parent. He was always doing what he wanted. Since the oldest three were with their father half the time most of it happened while they were gone. I was living in a constant state of flight or fight. I walked on eggshells and did everything I could to make him love me and not want to fight with me. No one knew how alone I felt and what I was going through.

One night, while all the kids were home, I came home to find him drunk with a friend because they got off work early. When that friend's wife called me to see if her husband was there I told her yes and that they were drunk. After he left, my husband got in my face and asked me why I told her that. I said because she asked me and she had a right to know. He was furious. It escalated quickly from there. Yelling, screaming, broken furniture, slaps, pushes, punches.

I defended myself the best I could, but I ran and locked myself and the kids in their room and we hid in the closet.

With them screaming and crying, I called my uncle up the street and told him to come and bring his gun. I thought we were going to have to kill him to get him to stop. My uncle and my cousin's husband came and they fought him to the ground. In the meantime, the police showed up. We came out of the bedroom and the deputies were talking to both of us. One of the deputies knew us, knew my husband's reputation and told me technically he could take me in, too. My husband had scratches on him, but my injuries were more severe so the deputy took him instead, but I had to go to the hospital and I had to press charges.

I called my ex to pick up our three kids and had to hear him lecture me, too. I know I deserved it, but I was defeated. I felt like I couldn't go on anymore. Ironically, my husband's cousin had come by after all this happened just for a visit and ended up being the one that drove me to the hospital. I had knots and bumps all over my head, a swollen face, scratches, and bruises.

I spent that night at my sisters; I just couldn't go back to that house. The next few days were a blur. I know I cried so much and felt so alone. No one seemed to care what I was going through. Fast forward, yes, I cried and begged him to come back and work it out. I didn't press charges and I went right back onto that hamster wheel. It was my normal. I only knew how to function like that. I was broke and broken all at the same time.

More years passed, more violence, more drinking and dui's, wrecked cars, other women, broken promises, and lies. So many lies. I thought I had worked out the perfect plan for us. If he was going to drink, I would drive him to the bar and when he was done I would pick him up. That way he wouldn't get into any trouble and he would be home at night with me. Boy, that worked out so well (sarcasm)...

The proverbial straw that broke the camel's back came when one of those nights I was called out of bed at 2 am and I headed to town to pick him up. When I got there, he got in the car and we started home. He had a habit of taking his hand and wiping it on my face from the forehead down to my chin to annoy me when I was driving. He did it this time and by the third time I bit his hand because I couldn't see the road and was scared I was going to wreck. We got to the stoplight and he looked at me and punched me three times hard right in the face. I turned the car around and drove straight to the police station and I said, "Get out of my car and go turn yourself in or I will." He finally got out of the car and took off walking. I wanted to walk through that door and press charges so bad, but was so scared of all the possibilities of what would happen when or if I walked in that door, that I turned the car around and went home.

He showed up sometime the next day. It was that moment when his fist struck my nose that I said enough. I woke up. No matter how long it took I made up in my mind that I was going to get out of this. It took me almost six months.

One night we had a family meeting and I had the kids tell him what they didn't like about his drinking. I hoped it would shame him into quitting. I said quit or get out. He packed a bag that night and walked out. I was a crying mess on the kitchen floor. Why did I care about someone who obviously didn't give a damn about me or our family? So I got up, put on a brave face and planned my out.

I left my house, my stuff, and in financial ruin I walked away. I could not have done it without his cousin, the one that took me to the hospital. He gave me money for rent/deposit and I was able to leave with somewhere to go to. I'd like to say that it ended there, but no. For the next year he stalked me, broke into my new home, stole my keys, stole all the items in my home that meant something to me, stole Christmas presents, stole my bras and panties because without them I couldn't go out or go to work, but I kept on going.

I filed for divorce and custody. He would come by and pretend he was going to sign the papers and then try to get in my house; he hit me again and spit in my face. I called the police. Every single time he touched me or did something to me, I called the police. I knew we had to have a record of it.

He had stripped me of all my dignity and self-esteem, but I was alive and I had my kids. I had protective order after protective order. He would violate it, go to jail, and get out and do it again. I feared for my life. He had always threatened me that he could shoot me, like a sniper, and I would never see it coming. I always looked over my shoulder. I had to break my lease and move more than once because he wouldn't leave me alone. I even pleaded with my landlord to let me out of my lease and I told him why and he said sorry I can't do that so I moved to a new apartment and broke that lease and they sued me.

It started again. When I was leaving my second home he actually came to the door on my moving day and said I guess you're breaking this lease, too. Then, he followed me to my third home. I couldn't escape him no matter what I tried. So after a few months I tried to flip the script and I started being nice to him. He would call me for a ride to cash his paycheck and I would take him and make him buy my groceries. I made him give me gas money. Anything, I could do to make it feel like it was a victory and that I could manipulate him like that. I never slept with him, but I did tell him I had met someone else and was dating him. He left me alone, but still wanted to see our son. After many failed attempts of him not seeing our son on his days I filed and was awarded full custody. I had won! Boy, was I naïve. At this time, I had been convinced to move into a house I couldn't afford, I was behind on all my bills and working a full and part-time job to make ends meet. There was never enough money.

Enter husband number three…I experimented with online dating during the time that I felt like I was in control of my life by being nice to my ex. I went through a phase that one could only call a promiscuous stage. I was careless and hooked up with lots of men. I thought I was single and carefree and could do anything I wanted for the first time in my life. Boom!! Reality hits and my downward spiral began.

I was in debt way over what I was making. My utilities were being shut off. I had to borrow money until there was no one left to borrow from. During this time I met my third husband. His profile looked harmless enough, divorced dad of two and successful enough. So my girlfriend convinced me to go to dinner with him. That was in November and that was the beginning of the last ten years of my life.

A month later we had our first date. It was one that you could dream about. He was gentlemanly, respectful, and showed me such a great time. We toured a winery, something I had never done, we went to dinner at a fancy restaurant and in the parking lot before dinner he kissed me. It was sweet, nice, and I loved the attention. Dinner was great and he showed me around the area where he lived because it was over an hour away from my home. Actually across a mountain. That became his favorite saying, "she's from the other side of the mountain". Similar to "the other side of the tracks".

We made out in his car that night and I refused to go to his house. I told him I wasn't sleeping with him on the first date. I was so proud of myself for that. Turns out that became a challenge for him. We spent that New Year's Eve together. He came over and we got a hotel room. We had a great time.

From that point on we were dating whenever we had the time. Weeknights, weekends, whenever. I drove the hour drive to see him and spend the night. How I didn't see the red flags is beyond me. I was always the one going to him. During one of the first times I went over I wore a pair of pajama pants because it was late and when he saw me he got angry and said don't you ever wear those again. When you come to see me you must be dressed properly. I felt like a scolded kid. I should have run, but I didn't.

Fast forward to a month later and I was laid off of my job. So no job, no money, I lost my house; my son and I were about to go live with my sister when he said, "Why don't you and your son move in with me?" "Just your son." My oldest lived with her boyfriend, my daughter and my other son would stay with their dad because of school. So I uprooted my baby boy, again, and moved him to a new school in a matter of days.

He was lost. New town, no friends. I felt like I was a horrible mother. I thought I was providing for him by making this move. In fact, I was hurting both of us, but we really had no choice. We would have been homeless. I thought I knew what I was doing. I always said that I married for love the first two times and the next time would be for security. I got my security, but at what cost?

He told me that I didn't have to work. He liked having me home when he got off and I could just take care of the house and do the yard work. What he really meant was now he had a hired hand that he didn't have to pay, that would do anything to pay her way to live in his house. I worked my butt off always trying to please him. I did everything his way and never stood up to him or questioned anything.

He started with little things; like, "I like blonde hair, why don't you dye your hair?" I did put in highlights and then little by little he nagged and nagged until I was a platinum blonde. He had me eat what he said. I lost weight down to the size he thought I should be. He bought my clothes. He told me what body wash I could use, which toothpaste. He made a schedule up of what I was to do with my day and if it took longer than he thought I was chastised. He turned me into the blonde Barbie doll that he wanted. He was king and he would tell you this.

I thought I had found my blessing. Sex, the sex was great, and then he started being adventurous and I went along with it, but it turned out I didn't like a lot of the things he wanted me to do. I felt dirty, and cheap. He demanded sex every single night. For the first five years we were together we may have only not had sex a handful of times. I was exhausted. Up late having sex and then working my ass off all day and doing it over and over. I really think it's one of the reasons today I no longer like it.

The red flags were screaming at me and I was too blind to see them. For once in my life I didn't have to worry about if we had heat, or food, or a roof over our heads. Years, I went blindly forward not realizing what this was doing to me or my family. Even being only an hour away, I was isolated from my family by a mountain. I only saw them when he said I could take his car to go visit, but I had to be back at whatever time he told me so that I could do whatever chore he had cooked up for me that day. I was once again alone.

His daughters hated me because they thought I took their dad away. The oldest even said that the only reason he was with me was because I would sleep with him. It was a bad time for everyone in the house. Those first few months he led me to believe he was so well off and we could do whatever we wanted. By February we were engaged and then married by July. I don't feel like I ever really knew him. His family was skeptical of us being together and made me feel like I didn't belong. But not him, he defended me and told them accept me or else. To this day I feel like only a handful of them actually like me. Everyone thought I was a gold-digger. Well, there had to be gold for that to happen.

It was 2008 and the recession hit. He was in over his head. All throughout this time, my ex was bombarding my current with pictures he had of me, a video, and texts. It was so bad. I can't really remember why he stopped, but he did one day. At this time my current decided we needed to move to Florida. So he walked away from his house, filed bankruptcy, found a job in Florida and moved me and my son as far away from everyone as he could. My youngest daughter decided to come with us and I thank God every day that she did. I was alone in a new place with no friends and she was there for me. We lived in Florida for two years and money was always tight. He went from job to job and I had only a part-time job that he allowed me to get finally.

How do I write about everything I went through? I start typing and one memory leads me to another memory and I feel like I should write them down in the hopes that they will help someone else, but then I feel like it's too much. This isn't supposed to be a story about all the examples of the things my narcissist has tried to do to gaslight me and manipulate me, but then again, isn't it? If the memories I write about are red flags and someone else reads them, won't that help them to see their own red flags?

I remember how out of my element I felt moving so far away. I had never been this far from my family in my whole life. Since I have a large family there is always someone sick, injured, dying, getting married, having kids, etc. and I wanted to be there for it. My current told me that I had to accept that I wasn't going to be able to go back and that if anybody died I had three funerals that I was allowed to come home for. He told me I had to pick the three that meant the most to me. How? Who gave him the right to tell me that I couldn't go to a family or friend's funeral? How, because he controlled our finances. He knew how much money we had and we didn't have a lot, but I knew if the situation arose I could count on others to help get me home.

It was things like this that made me trapped. I was not allowed to go on girl trips. He said that was just a bunch of married women wanting to mess around. I wasn't allowed to have male friends or speak to them outside of work. No male friends on social media. He was even jealous when my male cousin called me to check on my mother. He hated everyone in my family. I think that was from jealousy because we are all very close and he didn't have a close family. He never wanted to come to any family gathering unless he absolutely had no choice, but to do so.

Shifting back to our financial situation, it was getting worse and we had no health insurance so when his old job in Virginia (VA) wanted him back we moved back. This time we moved to a small town still over an hour away from my family. My daughter stayed in Florida. I was crushed to leave her. For the first three months back we had to live in the basement of the mother of a friend of his. It was winter, cold, dreary and I hated our life.

After three months, we finally had money again and we were able to rent a house. We now had insurance and that was about when his health started to be a problem. While we were in Virginia, he had to have his neck fused. He was in pain from previous back surgeries and now this. He took opioids daily, which he had been on for 10 years when I met him and still drank. He hated to be back in the cold and wanted to move back to Florida, again. It was a constant struggle.

During these periods he would do something nice, but I believe it all came back to control. My youngest son had come out and while we were both accepting him being gay, his bio dad was not. Here in lies a crossover. Dealing with my ex and my current. Two different types of abusers.

My ex called and spoke to my current about our son and asked him can't you beat the gay out of him? He told him to send him back that his father would take him to church and pray it out of him. He refused to have a gay son. My current decided he was going to adopt him and we went through the process and now he is our son. He loves him, but he can't control him.

After two years, we packed another U-Haul and back we went to Florida. During all this time, I was still being subjected to the constant ways of a narcissist. I think you finally become used to them. I can't pinpoint the exact decline, but he started to become worse. Health wise and narcissistic wise. It was his way or the highway. If I went anywhere and he couldn't reach me, he would scream and throw a fit when I returned. I had to go to bed when he did, wake up when he did, answer his calls immediately, only do the things he liked to do.

On and on and on…so many little things like this that I can't name them all. One example sticks out though. In 2017, Hurricane Irma was coming. We anxiously waited and wondered if we should evacuate. Not him he was excited. He told me we were staying. I said I didn't know if I wanted to and he told me to go, but he manipulated me to make me feel like leaving was not the right thing to do, so I stayed. We were able to shelter up in the school that he teaches in and along with us we brought my daughter, grandson, and son-in-law, as well as several friends and their spouses.

As the storm hit and we rode it out, all was good until they started talking about the surge. We were in the surge area and his classroom that we were staying in was on the first floor. We were given permission to move our things to a room upstairs and so everyone decided to do this, except him. I moved all of our stuff upstairs and as I was coming back down he came running down the hallway at me with this look on his face that I can't even describe. It was full rage and he didn't care who was there. He started screaming at me in front of everyone how he didn't give me permission to move his stuff and he wanted all of it put back downstairs and how everyone else were pu**ies for moving upstairs.

I dragged him to an empty room where he continued to scream at me and degrade me. I cried and told him that I couldn't do this anymore. He didn't care. I think that night the last little bit I was holding onto was gone. Later that night we were discussing what we were going to do when the storm was over. Everyone was anxious to see what damage had been done to their property. I was in another area of the school and had missed this discussion. As I was walking back to our area, one of my friends came up to me crying and telling me that my current had told her she was not allowed to leave until we had cleaned everything up. As he had the key to the gate and she wouldn't be able to get her car out without it. I couldn't believe that he had said this and made her cry. He knew how upset everyone was due to this storm. I found him and I blasted him good for it. For once I must have gotten through to him because he actually came in the room and had a conversation with my friend and apologized sincerely. But it was too little too late. I had seen the monster he was and I was done. My heart started to harden that day.

My health wasn't ever really bad, but about a year after we were married I ended up having a hysterectomy and bladder tack. Then came the migraines. He didn't understand how a headache could make you not function until I was at the Dr. for a recheck from my hysterectomy and my ob/gyn asked me what was wrong. I told her I had a headache that was a 13 on the pain scale and that at lunch that day I was speaking in gibberish. She went across the hall and found a doctor that would see me immediately. The doctor examined me and told me that she was admitting me. They thought I had a stroke.

I called him at work and said they won't let me leave and either you have to drive me or they will call an ambulance. He drove me to the hospital where I underwent a barrage of tests that determined I didn't have a stroke, but a rebound migraine. I was in the hospital for a week. I got out and still had the headache. Three days later I had an appointment with a neurologist. She was my saving grace. She took me off everything they had me on and put me on two different medicines and by the second day my headache was gone.

I started to have different issues after that. Many urinary tract infections, especially since I was still coerced into having sex on a daily basis. He didn't understand how these issues would interfere with our sex life. It was a year after we moved to Florida that I was diagnosed with Fibromyalgia. If any of you know anything about it, there are over 200 symptoms and many autoimmune diseases that come from having it. So begins my health journey.

Right from the beginning he didn't believe the diagnosis and to this day he doesn't. He believes that I don't have pain as bad as his and that I need to "suck it up" just like he does. I developed Irritable Bowel Syndrome-Diarrhea and Interstitial Cystitis, bladder condition. All this paired with the Fibromyalgia and my libido took a nose dive. Oh and yes, mother menopause came knocking.

I underwent surgery for the IC and was implanted with a device to help contract the bladder so that issue is manageable, but does flare up. So now here I am, 51 years old, overweight, no sex drive, in pain every day, and married to a narcissist that thinks the world revolves around him. So moving forward….I must have "woke up" as they say and decided I needed to be me again.

In February of this year (2019), I went to my hair stylist and told her to color my hair red. When she was done and I looked in the mirror I almost cried. I didn't recognize that woman. She had been gone for sooo many years and now here she was staring back at me saying ok now what? I drove home and walked in the house and he had his back to me. I said you may as well get it over with because I colored my hair and you aren't going to like it. He turned around and that moment I saw evil in his eyes. He flipped out. The worst I have ever seen. He called me so many names, told me I had to "fix it" and it had to be done in one day or else. He told me he couldn't stand to look at me. That I made him sick to his stomach. I stood strong and stood up to him and I think that was the moment he knew he no longer had control over me.

He was so mad he stormed out of the house and ended up sitting in his truck for hours. He couldn't leave because as usual he had been drinking and he was a staunch believer in not drinking and driving. So he sat. That began the worst four days of my life. From the moment I would get home from work until bed he belittled me, degraded me, cussed me, and yelled at me, you name it. By the fourth day he just shut himself off from me.

We have basically been living in our house like roommates ever since that day. Fast forward to April and he has a student that he had to take to a competition for 5 days 4 nights. While he is away I decided to do a little investigating. He isn't a social media wiz so the only form of communication he has is his phone. I went online to our phone records and there I found that he had been communicating with a number I didn't recognize. I Googled the number and found out it was an old girlfriend of his from high school. I sent him a text and told him that I found out and we went back and forth arguing via text all day.

That evening when he got back to his room we were on the phone for an hour and of course it was all my fault. He did nothing wrong because it wasn't physical. I guess I lost it and was so upset I was hysterical and inconsolable. When he returned home he said that sex was a big part of a relationship to him and that I took it away from him. Not because I have a medical condition that is incurable and painful, but because I just decided I didn't want to have sex anymore.

I defended myself by saying that I can have sex we just have to do certain things and it can't be as often as he wants (daily or at minimum every other day). He said that was unacceptable. That I pushed him to do what he did and that it wasn't wrong because he hadn't been physical with her. He could understand how it would upset me, but that he didn't think it was a big deal. I asked him if it had been me what would you have done? He said you would be out on the street. So therein lies the question, why is it ok for him to do that to me, but not me to him? Narcissistic much?? He is a class A, covert, grandiose narcissist.

So for the past two weeks since I found out it has seemed like a year. I feel like I'm grieving a death. In a way, I am. The death of the idea of what we meant to each other. He has continued to stay in contact with his new supply all the while still asking me for sex, sleeping next to me every night, and kissing me goodbye every morning with an I love you have a great day. The emotional rollercoaster is so bad. I'm drained of all energy and feel so defeated. I hate him and I love him.

My heart hurts and then my heart hardens and I'm glad he is someone else's problem. He has no empathy and he claims that our impending divorce is all my fault because I could have "fixed" the problem, but I chose not to. The "fix" he refers to is that I start having sex every day with him and I color my hair back blonde and lose weight. Then I will be the perfect wife. I guess I will die alone because I will not subject myself to that anymore. As soon as I am financially able, I am out of this toxic situation and I will then start the road back to healing myself once again only this time wiser and not as naïve. If I make it this time I vow to never put myself back into an abusive relationship again. I will educate myself on the red flags to look for and stand up for myself. I am someone, I am valuable, I am worth it, I AM ME!

"A journey of a thousand miles begins with a single step."

Journey 12

Jezebel's Daughter

As a child, I never imagined not having both of my parents actively in my life. My mother was a drug addict and an alcoholic. My father was ambivalent. They were young and had no clue about the dedication, commitment, and sacrifices that it would take to raise a child. My mother put many things in front of me, such as her drugs, men, and partying. It appears nothing was ever about making sure that my safety and well- being was ever a priority.

If it were not for my grandparents stepping in to make sure that a lot of my basic needs were taken care of, I would have been at a total loss. I know my gran'mommy prayed for me for many years. It is because of her prayers that I became the woman who I am today. My gran'daddy passed away when I was 10 years old.

I can remember my father's wife braiding my hair with extensions. I already knew how to plat. After my father's wife learned it, she taught me, amazingly. Interestingly, I braided my first head at the tender age of 10 years old. It was awful. It was my work and I was proud of it. My aunt, who has never braided hair a day in her life, showed me a trick. She showed me how to make the braids so that they lined up neatly along the hairline. By this time, I was approximately 14 years old. Braiding hair would soon become a passion and a business, for me.

I was home for a visit, from San Diego, California, where I lived with my other aunt. During my first year of high school, I attended Mount Carmel in Rancho Penasquitos in San Diego County. For some reason, my mother wanted me to come back home with her to Buena Park. I was enrolled in Western High School in Anaheim. My mother sent me to live with my father the following year after a Halloween party and a fight had broken out. She had promised me that she was going to give me $100 to go shopping at the Buena Park Mall. The Buena Park Mall is in Buena Park, California, near Knott's Berry Farm. We lived around the corner from there.

My aunt came into the room where all of the children were and asked me, "Why is your face so long?" I explained, "I know my momma isn't going to give me the money that she promised. She never does." My aunt went to ask my mother about it. Suddenly, my mother snapped, and they started fighting. I was terrified because I had never experienced anything like that.

My mother called my father and told him that he had to come and get me. This man was some kind of stranger to me. I mean, I knew him somewhat better as a little child. I was 15 years old, liking boys and actually had a boyfriend. He took me home with him to his apartment on Mulberry Street in Compton, California. It was a huge change from living with my mother. I had no privacy, no freedom, and suddenly I wasn't the only child in the home. I had to share, which wasn't a problem. However, my step-sister wasn't used to new clothing and having a lot of brand-new things. Her mother shopped at the second hand store, a lot. Thus, there was some envy there. I loved second hand store shopping too, but my mother forbid to shop in second hand stores, although she failed to provide me with decent and clean clothing.

Nonetheless, I started school at Dominguez High School, in Compton, in 1986. The teachers were on strike that year. There were hardly any classes to go to and rarely was homework ever given. So, I ditched every day with my classmates. I ended up meeting a guy, who was doggy doggish. He asked me to hang with him one day and I agreed. It was March 31, 1987. I had just turned 16 years old a couple of months prior. I thought it was all in my mind that he was this way. Turns out, he was showing me just who he really was. He took me behind an abandoned house and told me that he was going to have sex with me. My heart dropped beneath my feet. I had no idea what to do. I just knew that I wasn't prepared for anything like this. After disagreeing with his idea, he literally told me that I was either going to give it up or he was taking it. I knew then, the fight was on. Eventually, he won the fight and tied me down and had his way with me. I was so afraid to tell. I knew my father was going to preach to me and tell me that I was going to hell. Therefore, I kept it to myself. I took a bath and tried to put it out of my mind. I went to school the next day and there he was… waiting for me. He grabbed my hand and I took off running. I am not sure what happened after that, but I had never seen him again.

Most of my peers were sexually active. I felt so weird. I felt like something was wrong with me, but I didn't want to do it again. I took myself to class and didn't ditch anymore. I made up work to do just so that I could keep myself busy. I asked to be changed to Home Economics so that I could learn to sew. I met some nice girls in that class. I also met my second hair client. She paid me $40 to French braid her a ponytail. It took me about 8 hours to complete it. She loved it. More people wanted me to braid their hair.

My father's wife didn't want me braiding hair at home. The end of the school year was approaching. My father and his wife asked me about my report card. I hadn't received it. They were the type of people where everything had to be exaggeratedly dramatized. They would talk to us for hours, repeating themselves, and never getting a solid point across. So, I lied to them often in hopes that it would curtail a good bit of the conversation. Well it didn't. It seemed to make it worse. So I decided to tell the truth. That didn't help, either. I was damned if I did and damned if I didn't.

Sometimes these talks would go on for three… four… five… and even six hours. Well, this was one of those times where the conversation was about six hours. They kept asking why I stole my report card. No matter what I said, they didn't believe me. Heck, they never believed me when I told the truth, which is why I decided to lie in the first place. They went to the school and spoke to my guidance counselor, who told it all. "Yep, she has been ditching. She hasn't been in most of her classes. We require all of the children to still attend classes even though there are no teachers in them," my guidance counselor told my father and his wife. She promised them that they mailed my report card to the address on file. I was then accused of breaking in the mailbox. You know the one that the postman has to have a key to open when he is putting mail in multiple mailboxes for an apartment unit? Yeah, that one. I was never around when the mailman delivered the mail. How in <u>THEE</u> world would I get the mail? I didn't know about breaking into anything.

Ironically, sometimes, they would believe my lies. However, when it came to my report card, I told the entire truth. They still did not believe me. My father told me that he was going to beat me because he knew that I was lying. His wife said, "I will hold her so that you can beat her behind. She is gonna learn to stop lying to us today." His wife locked my head between her knees and my father pulled my pants down and literally beat the breaks off of me. I had to sit on my hips because it hurt too badly to sit on my behind.

The last two weeks of school was hell for me. I had to go to summer school. The second day of summer school, my father had to go to court for child support for my brother. He was locked up for nonpayment. It was that day that I decided that I was going to run away, and I was not going back to that hell hole with those crazy people. I ran away to my mother. My father's wife claimed that she went looking for me and that she couldn't sleep. Whatever her case is or was, it wasn't going to involve me anymore.

When I ran away, I went to a neighborhood across the street from the Compton courthouse on Palmer Street. I went to my cousin's house and met my mother there. When I showed them what was left of the bruising on my butt cheeks, they wanted to go fight my father's wife. I didn't want them to do that because despite how rude and evil she had been to me, I didn't have the heart to go tit for tat and have her beaten up.

I re-enrolled at Western High School, in Anaheim. I was now in the 11th. My friends and I were excited to see one another, again. They set me up to braid their hair. It was three of them and two of them wanted braids. My cousins tried getting me clients from Orange Jr. High School. It wasn't but a handful of us, so we really valued one another, even though the braiding business was sparse. We lived with my aunt who had fought my mother over the $100. I didn't have school clothes for the upcoming school year. My gran'mommy couldn't help me that year because she had a fixed income. Living with my aunt was about as bad as living with my father. I just had a little more freedom. She would make statements, such as, "Don't nobody eat this food. It is for my daughter and my daughter only.

There were other children in the home. No, we weren't her children and she didn't feed us either. My mother wouldn't complete the lunch form so that I could at least receive free lunch at school. I spent a lot of days hungry. One day in particular, I asked her for $2 so that I could eat lunch. She yelled at me and said, "Gott dammit, I ain't got no f***in' $2. Take yo ass to school and leave me alone." She had been drinking and she had been up getting high.

I was starving. My stomach and my back were playing tag. I left out of the door and slammed it. It was a heavy bar door. She ran out after me and started choking me by my hoodie. She was yelling while I was trying to catch my breath. I went to school in tears. I hated school. I couldn't learn. I didn't feel smart. And, I hated the world. My mother had a husband. He was just as much of a nuisance as everyone else. He was a chronic cheater, thief, and definitely came with a notarized tongue that was stamped "LIAR." He moved away to his home town, Phenix City, Alabama. In the midst of this, I had two little brothers who were shipped off to my mother's husband's family in Phenix City. Eventually, she followed right behind him, leaving me with my aunt.

I tried pushing my hair game really hard. I got tired of being hungry. My friends would help me find customers and they started coming, slowly, but surely. Then, my aunt got upset with me for leaving my makeup in the bathroom. I left it to go show my friends how my face looked. She was looking for any excuse to get rid of me and it worked. I ended up in Phenix City with my mother. She lived in the projects. They were really nice and nothing like the projects in California. I spent two months there in the summer of 1988.

My mother was talking about leaving me to go back to California to remove the items from her storage. I convinced her to allow me to go. She finally agreed. My friends had a huge lineup for me. I literally made the money to pay for her storage, get my bus ticket, and have money for food while traveling. Once I arrived in California and made my money, it was stolen from me. I believe it was one of the crack-head relatives. Either way, this further damaged the relationship between my mother and I. She called me everything, but her child and a child of God. Her sister, the one who used to live in San Diego, tried to explain it to her. She wasn't trying to hear it. She told me to call their family friend and ask him if he had the money to help me get back. He agreed to do it in exchange for a sexual favor. I thought I was going to puke. This man was old enough to be my granddaddy. He had a belly the size of an elephant's behind. SEXUAL FAVOR??? Ewe! I was stuck y'all. I wasn't going to do it. It wasn't a figment of my imagination.

I ended up being sent back to my father's place. Because we were under the impression that I was going back to Alabama from what my mother told us, they never enrolled me in the 12th grade. I missed everything. The 12th grader's dream of finishing strong was something that I never got. I felt as though my life was over. No one really cared. Here I was 18 years old. No formal education. No job. No clientele. Just nothing.

By the end of September 1989, I was pregnant with my first child. In December 1989, I went to someone's home in Riverside, California, to braid hair. I was given me a ride there, but they wouldn't take me back home, after I braided the client's hair and gave her a discount for transporting me. The lady even threw me out of her house and accused me of wanting her boyfriend. I had never met this man and had never seen him prior to that moment. I was furious.

I went to the payphone and tried calling everyone in my family. The only person I reached was a cousin who lived in Fresno, California. She tried calling everyone on three-way. Oddly, no one answered. It was December 14th, approximately 11 pm. I asked my cousin to call my baby's father, as she did so many times while I was on the phone. He finally answered. I asked him to please come and get me. He said, "I didn't get you there and I ain't gettin' you back." He hung the phone up in my face. Then the unbelievable happened. It was truly an unimaginable moment.

Four men drove up in a car. I was forced to go with these guys. I was told that my new name was *"Bitch"* and that I was gonna f*** all of their friends. I was held at knife point and my life was threatened. I was made to ride in the backseat naked. I was cold, shaking, and deathly afraid. Prayer was my best friend in this hour. The last of the four guys said, "Aye! I ain't had my turn." I begged him to pretend. He said, "I can't let the homies down. I gotta do it for my homies." Tears rolled from my eyes as I laid there. I felt worthless. I felt as though my dignity had been stolen. I felt like a piece of trash.

Finally, the man who owned the car dropped the other three guys off to their designated locations. My brain was so tired, but I couldn't fall asleep. I didn't know what I would have awakened to. Nonetheless, the guy couldn't figure out what to do with me. He told me that he was taking me home with him. He told me up front that I better be obedient. He said, "You better do as I say and you will be alright."

I was super nervous. I had no idea what I was walking into. He introduced me to his girlfriend and their two sons. My heart literally sank into my stomach. How in the world was this monster living with himself? His girlfriend was of Asian descent. She handed me some cover and asked my name. Before I could answer, he said, "She is my homeboy's sister. They got into a fight so I told her that she could stay here with us for the night." She reached to shake my hand. I didn't want to let her hand go as it was a plea for help. In my mind I thought, "Does this happen with them all of the time? Could she be oblivious to her man's antics with other females? Does she know that he is a rapist?" As nice as she seemed, I knew that if I did anything out of the norm that he set for me, it could mean my life would be taken from me.

She handed me the phone and said, "If you need to call anyone, feel free to use the phone. Make yourself at home." The guy came and sat next to me when she went back in the room. He said, "Don't you dare try anything funny. I will f*** you up. F*** you and that baby. It ain't mine so I don't care. Call your peoples and tell them that you ain't nev'a comin' back home because you are now my bitch." He finally closed the door.

My heart was beating a million miles per minute. I had no clue what to think or do. All I knew to do was pray. I asked God to please deliver me out of that situation alive and to protect my little baby. I picked up the phone and called 911. When the agent answered, she said, "911, what's your emergency? I told her that I had been kidnapped and raped. She immediately asked for the name of a close friend. Jackie. I couldn't think of another name. She said, "Hey girl. This is Jackie. How are you doing?" She advised me to follow along in the event that someone picked up another phone. I wasn't sure if there was another phone or not. Therefore, I followed her lead. I looked at the clock. It was 3:25 AM.

The conversation continued. I couldn't help but to think about my unborn baby and how much time I might have left... or not have left. She asked if I was bleeding at all. I wasn't sure. She asked me to find the bathroom. I was able to see the bathroom from where I was sitting. I tiptoed in there to see if there was any blood. Thankfully there wasn't. I was extremely sore and hurting in my woman parts. I tiptoed back to the phone. I told her that there was no blood. She asked me if I wiped myself. I told her that I did. She said, "If you have to go to the bathroom again, DO NOT wipe yourself. I know is sounds gross. I will explain it to you later. So did you know why my momma named me Jackie?" I had to keep remembering to follow her lead. She said, "I am going to count to three. When I do, slowly walk out the door and go hide behind the first car that you see." I had no clue where she was talking about. However, I was ready to be freed from that situation.

I tiptoed over to the door. The handle made some noise. I hurried and grabbed the phone and told her that I couldn't do it. That little bit of noise could have set everything off. She told me to hold on. I looked at the clock. It was 3:45 AM. She came back to the phone and said, "When I count to three, you run out of the door as fast as you can and hide behind the cop car that will be right in front of you. I held my breath and waited for the count. She started, "One, two, three... GO!" I dropped the phone and ran as fast as I could out of the door. I saw police and guns hiding in the cut. No one was behind me. I ran and hid behind the cop car that was in front of me.

Before I could blink, police came out of everywhere with all guns drawn. They went into the house. There were two officers with me. The ambulance was there and Riverside County Fire Department was there. One of the guys from the ambulance asked, "Do you want to go to the hospital?" I responded, "Yes." He commented, "I don't know why you want to go…" I immediately cut him off and said, "First of all, I need to see if my unborn baby is alright for if I am having a miscarriage. I was raped by four guys!" They brought the man out in handcuffs. I had no clue that he was intoxicated to the extent that he was. His girlfriend gave the police the story that he gave her. I was his homeboy's sister. I had no clue who any of these guys were and I definitely had no clue about his homeboy or the sister. Once that was clarified, I was transported to Riverside County Regional Medical Center in Riverside, California.

The emergency room Physician conducted a sexual assault forensic exam. He said that he found semen from my hair to the bottom of my feet. Three of the guys actually ejaculated. The other guy didn't. However, they were able to match him by hair follicles. The arresting officer and a rape crisis counselor had to be in the exam room with me. It was extremely painful. The physician said that I had a lot of torn skin in my genitalia. The physician's report was submitted to the police. The Riverside County Sheriff called it gang rape or rape in concert.

The whole sordid ordeal was a nightmare. I had to go on a route with the detective. I was able to recall every place that they had taken me the night before. The guys saw me in the car with the detective and they ran for dear life. Two additional arrests were made within a week. The fourth guy was on the run. I had to go to court and testify. I went through this alone. I had no one to go with me. I was terrified. I knew I had to do it and I did. I had nightmares. I woke up in cold sweats. I couldn't eat some days, which wasn't healthy for my baby.

Finally, I had my baby and dug deep into the healing process. I built my hair clientele and took care of us. Her father was just as bad as my father. Nonetheless, my baby didn't go without and I vowed to give her a better life than what was handed to me by my parents. I was directionless. I was judged for having two STD's from a situation that I wasn't a willing participant in.

If I never learn anything else in life, I learned to stand up for my children. When people know and see that you don't care, your child will be mistreated. Jezebel left her daughter by the wayside. To be continued.....

"You had the power all along my dear."

About the Authors

Daria Wilkes

Daria is originally from Glendale, California. After living in California, Illinois, Texas, and Georgia her family settled in suburban Baltimore in the late 80s. She has lived an adventure of a life with many wonderful, and many terrible experiences. She has experienced everything from flying in a traffic helicopter over downtown St. Louis at nine years of age, and a hot air balloon race at sixteen, to more concerts and music festivals than she can count, and the births of her children. She's also lived through the deaths of close friends, brutal battles with mental illness, and twenty years with an abusive narcissist. Above all, she got to see that life is an experience worth having.

She credits a career in competitive gymnastics in her youth for her toughness, and unwillingness to give up. She is now happily married to a wonderful man that gives her flowers for no reason, and living peacefully in a suburban state with her family.

Donyelle Allen

Donyelle Allen is an anointed inspirational mentor who specializes in discipleship. In 2017, she created "Women Shining Bright" a place for women to come and receive daily inspiration through devotions, positive self-talk affirmations, and inspirations.

As a young woman, Donyelle found herself stuck in a place of darkness. Filled with disappointment, frustration, and had lost hope, she felt lost, alone, and overlooked. It was in that place God allowed her to see something greater - the love He had for her true and unique self. Donyelle's life forever changed, giving her a new hope and a new love for God's people.

Donyelle is God's beloved daughter and has a passion for helping women overcome their dark places. She is a licensed nurse with a caring heart in California. She is a wife to an incredible husband, a mother to four amazing children, and a grandmother to a wonderful granddaughter. Her calling on Earth is to educate, encourage, and motivate people to reach their highest potential helping them to grow closer to God. In her free time she enjoys meditating and writing devotions. She also loves to dig deep into her creative side with making crafts.

Jamila Johnson

Jamila Johnson was born in Dallas, Texas, where she currently resides with her husband and three beautiful children. Jamila enjoys reading her Bible, shopping, crafts, and writing.

Her family attends church faithfully, where Jamila has gained a true relationship with Christ and discovered her gift is writing. Through writing, Jamila now understands that going through trials is a way she can help serve others and help bring them to Christ.

A scripture that Jamila reflects on through her trials and how she has triumphed over the enemy is John 3:16. She is a proud published author of *"The Embellishment of a Proverbs 31 Woman,"* a devotional for women. Jamila was a co-author in *Pretty* SAD Volume II and she is currently working on two book projects with expected released dates this year.

Katrina Turner Walker

Katrina Turner Walker is a Certified Relationship Life Coach and Published Author. She is currently a State Director for Wife Talk. Wife Talk is a non-profit organization with a mission to inspire, encourage and uplift married and engaged women.

Katrina was raised in East Chicago, Indiana. She currently resides in Florida with her husband of 28 years. They have one son, one Godson, and two grandsons. Katrina accredits her success to God, her husband, her sister and her deceased brother.

Katrina enjoys spending time with God, quality time with her family, hanging out with friends, meeting new people, traveling and helping women discover their worth.

Keci Monique

Keci Monique` Reynolds is a Vocational Consultant who is currently enrolled at Thomas University to earn a second Master's degree in Clinical Mental Health and Clinical Rehabilitation Counseling. She has a Bachelor's degree in Criminal Justice and a Master's degree in Forensic Psychology. She helps developmentally disabled persons to become rehabilitated and enter the workforce by means of vocational training, within a community work adjustment setting, educational means, job readiness, supported employment, and other services that can enable a feasible quality of life.

Before her employment as a Vocational Consultant, Keci worked as a Case Manager for Job Corps to work with at-risk youth and young adults. Aside from being a Detention Services Officer for Los Angeles County Probation, being a Case Manager was definitely a rewarding part of her career. Keci is also an entrepreneur and was a cosmetologist for over 30 years as a means of support for herself and her children. She currently has a t-shirt business and an event planning business. She is also in the process of establishing a non-profit to help females who are children of drug addicts, at-risk and other life complications.

Keci enjoys creating designs for her t-shirts, working on DIY projects, crocheting, sewing, and hanging out with family and friends. Keci is available for writing projects, as well as private consultations. She is a co-author in the soon-to-be released *Pretty* SAD Volume 4.

Latonya Littlejohn

Latonya is a mother and a wife. She is also a published author. Born Torie Michelle Kennedy, she was also born with conditions that would aim to plague her life: spina bifida and hydrocephalus, The Doctors placed limits on Latonya that she would eventually overcome.

She was born with a fighting spirit and although her name was changed after she was adopted, the fight in her remained. You can read more about her determination, her fight, and her will to live in her autobiography, "Delayed Not Denied." In her book, Latonya tells her story of meeting her biological family and overcoming a life that tried to stop her destiny. Latonya is a co-author in the soon-to-be released *Pretty* SAD Volume 4. She enjoys praise dance and writing. She is currently working on her second book, with an expected release this year.

Melissa McGill

Melissa McGill has been writing all of her life. She began writing her thoughts and adventures as a child in an effort to express herself and to remove herself from the not so pleasant environment she grew up in. Her dream is to write books that will uplift, inspire and encourage people all over the world.

Melissa is a Woman of God, a military wife of an active duty Command Master Chief of the U.S. Navy, a Mother of four wonderful children, of whom three are young adults, and she is a true lifelong friend to many people.

Melissa currently lives in Yokosuka, Japan with her husband, however, she is proud to call Charlotte, North Carolina home. She considers herself a southern lady who possesses all the charm, mannerism and hospitality of the culture of the Southern United States. When she isn't writing, she is active in her church serving as a Deaconess as well as serving in various other ministries.

She works full-time as an Administrative Assistant and is also a Paralegal. She is active in her community where she has served as a Command Family Ombudsman and currently serves as a member of the Triad Spouse Support Team. Melissa is the Director of the first overseas military chapter of Wife Talk Military Yokosuka, Japan where she is dedicated to uplifting and inspiring wives through the Word of God.

Melissa loves encouraging people with her writing, her words and her lifestyle. She uses the negative things she went through as a child to inspire others today to be positive overcomers rather than a product of their environment. Her vision and goal is to change the perception of negativity in the world one book at a time. She is the author of *Keep it Positive*, a book filled with wisdom and encouragement. Melissa is also a co-author in *Pretty* SAD Volume 2 and the soon-to-be-released Volume 4.

Pamela Southers

Pamela is 51 years young. She is a mother of four beautiful children (2 girls & 2 boys); stepmother to four, and LaLa to a spunky, adventurous, fun filled grandson.

She is originally from a small town in Virginia and now resides in Florida. She works as a Legal Assistant for a Family Lawyer and has had the ability to use her own experiences to help clients be comfortable in their situations. Having been a domestic violence survivor, not once, but three times in her life she has now found the courage to rebuild her life on her own terms and find out what her interests are and do the things that bring her joy.

Being a part of this project has been so therapeutic. Her hope is that by reading her story it will inspire others in the same situations to take charge of their lives and know that they are worthy of so much more. She would like to become more in involved as a domestic violence advocate with similar projects. The future has endless possibilities and she is going to explore as many as she can. Live, Laugh and Love!

Sinnika Gibbs

Sinnika is 32 years young. She resides in California, with her husband and two children. She is the oldest of 11 children; 3 sisters and 8 brothers. Family is very important to Sinnika and she spends as much time as possible with her family.

She attends church faithfully and holds a Bachelor's of Science degree in Psychology, with a minor in Sociology. Sinnika's goal is to obtain her Master's degree in Marriage and Family therapy. Her goal is to help others heal from past trauma, in order to to live full and happy lives.

Sinnika is the owner of A Breathtaking Occasion, and event planning and decorating company. In her personal time she likes to bake, crochet, craft, golf and play games with her family and friends.

Thea Herbert

Thea is a 34 year old single mom of four children. She is originally from the state of New York. She learned a lot from all of her relationships, especially the abusive ones. Now, Thea knows her entire worth and refuses to settle for less than she deserves.

Thea paints, draws, writes, and cooks. In her spare time, she loves working on DIY (do-it-yourself) activities and projects with her children. They are constantly finding new ideas and new recipes to try. Thea and her children are living everyday as if they have no fear, and even though it is still there, they believe that one day soon they will be able to live their lives without looking over their shoulders.

As a survivor, Thea has begun to help victims of abuse who reach out to her. She gives them resources in order to help them to get out of their abusive relationships. Her closest friends back her in every decision that she has made, and will continue to do so.

Tanya DeFreitas

Born in Pasadena, California, Tanya DeFreitas is the Lead Author of *Pretty* **SAD** and the Founder of the #TimetoTell movement. She is Founder of Love Wins Publishing, Women Who Write, and The Silent Warrior social & support group for married women.

Tanya is a self-published author, anthologist, and entrepreneur. A survivor of domestic violence and sexual assault, Tanya is also a certified Domestic Violence Advocate and supports the fight against abuse & sex trafficking.

Tanya has a passion for working with and helping women. She enjoys reading, speaking, traveling, and writing. She has more than 30 published works of her own, including workbooks, journals, inspirational devotions, self-help books and anthologies.

Tanya is a woman of faith. She was a single mother for more than 18 years. She is now married and resides in California, with her husband and children.

For more information about her published works, please check out her author page: Amazon.com/author/tanyadefreitas

Join the Movement

The Time to Tell movement was created by Tanya DeFreitas. Tanya is a survivor of domestic violence, sexual abuse, depression, suicide, and severe trauma. She created *Pretty* SAD in an effort to create a safe space to tell her own story of overcoming and she invited other women to join her. The first volume was intended to be a single book project and has since exploded into multiple books and a movement: #timetotell.

Time to Tell is about uncovering. It is about exposing secrets, shedding light on abuse & severe trauma, and the journey of healing. Survivors of abuse and severe trauma are often encouraged and/or expected to keep silent about their experiences. The #timetotell movement is about speaking up and speaking out. It is about exposing deep and dark secrets within families and within individuals.

Secrets are like cancer. They are an invasion to our lives and if left unexposed and unattended they will eventually spread causing more damage and issues. Their mission is to kill. They kill dreams, they kill purpose, they kill families, and they kill lives.

Join the movement and take a stand against keeping and holding onto to secrets and hurts of the past. It is time to tell the truth, the whole truth and nothing but the truth so help us God. And the truth shall set us free! #timetotell #themovement # *Pretty*SAD

For more information about the movement or any the following, please contact us:

- this book
- the authors who contributed to this book
- participating in the next volume of this book
- the publishing company
- speaking engagements

latanyadefreitas@gmail.com

Resources

Alcoholics Anonymous...www.aa.org

Gamblers Anonymous..................... www.gamblersanonymous.org

Overeaters Anonymous..www.oa.org

Child Abuse Hotline...1-800-422-4453

Cocaine Help Line 1-800-262-2463

Domestic Violence Hotline..1-800-799-7233

Drug/Alcohol Abuse...1-800-662-HELP

Eating Disorders Center 1-888-236-1188

Ecstasy Addiction..1-800-468-6933

HIV/AIDS National Hotline.......................................1-800-342-2437

National Teen Dating Abuse......................................1-866-331-9474

Rape, Abuse, Incest National Hotline...................1-800-656-4673

Runaway Hotline..1-800-621-4000

STD Hotline 1-800-227-8922

Suicide & Crisis Hotline 1-800-999-9999

Teen Helpline 1-800-400-0900

Teen Suicide Hotline...1-800-621-4000

Pretty SAD
Volume I & Volume II

If you enjoyed Volume III, you will absolutely love Volume I & II! *Pretty* SAD is an anthology that highlights the extraordinary strength of women. The stories in this collaboration are about struggle and survival, tragedy and triumph. These stories paint a clear picture of how a little girl can be broken and abused, grow up and make poor choices, yet still evolve into an incredible, phenomenal woman. In each volume, several women come together to share their stories

Available on Amazon.com

Coming soon…
Pretty SAD
Volume IV

Available July 2019

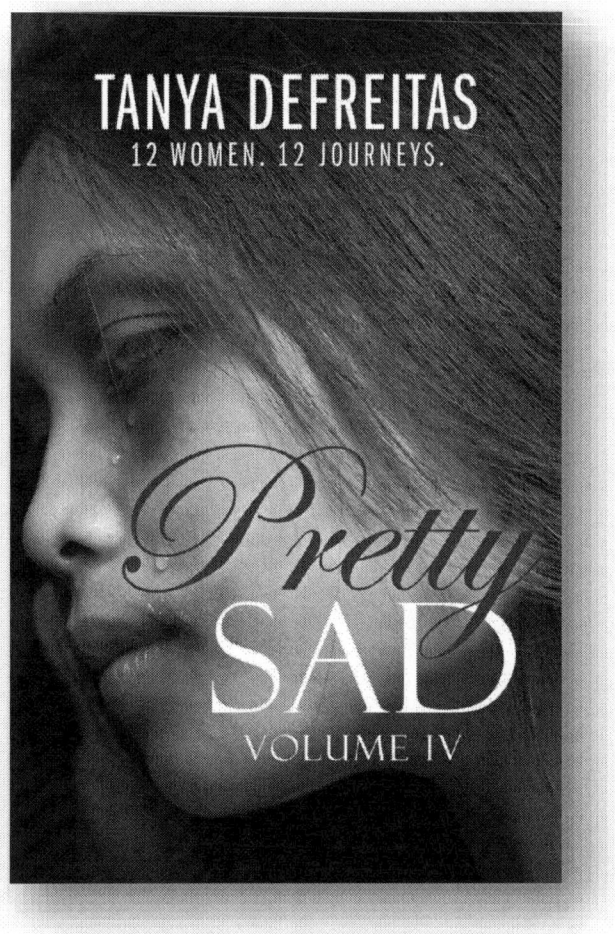

The following are books by the co-authors of *Pretty* SAD, Volume I –III and are available NOW on Amazon.com

The Embellishment of a Proverbs 31 Woman

By Jamila Johnson

In this gentle, yet thought-provoking devotional, Jamila Johnson shares bits & pieces of her own journey of becoming a virtuous woman. Jamila is married and struggled with adjusting to her role as a wife early on. Throughout the course of her life, Jamila learned that being virtuous is not out of reach. There is an inner beauty that is attainable for all women that can only be attained from the Heavenly Father. This devotional encourages women to look in the mirror and self-reflect, making adjustments where necessary.

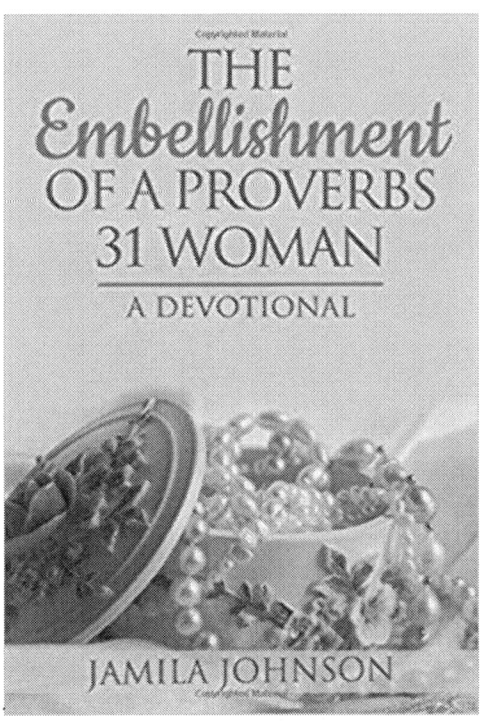

Scrapes and Scars

By Chavonne Hurdle

If you are running away from the demons of your past, here's the bitter truth: They will keep chasing you, and you will have to keep running forever. You just cannot outrun them. For every day that you hide your scars from the world, pretending like nothing happened, they dig just a little deeper into your soul.

Don't let the memories scar you for life. Speak up. Seek help. Heal what's been hurting you.

Read *Scrapes and Scars*, by Chavonne Hurdle, to follow the real life events of how a brave girl with terrible childhood memories took charge of her destiny and overcame her fears.

Keep it Positive

By Melissa McGill

Keep it Positive, by Melissa McGill, represents one mile of a journey she has been on, while trying to keep a positive attitude, in the midst of negativity.

"I had to live this book before I could write even one chapter. I choose to see the good in people, places and things. I choose to live a life free of drama, hate, chaos and foolishness even if it does occur all around me. I am a firm believer that if I encourage others, I will be encouraged too." Don't sweat the small stuff, keep it positive, even in the midst of negativity!

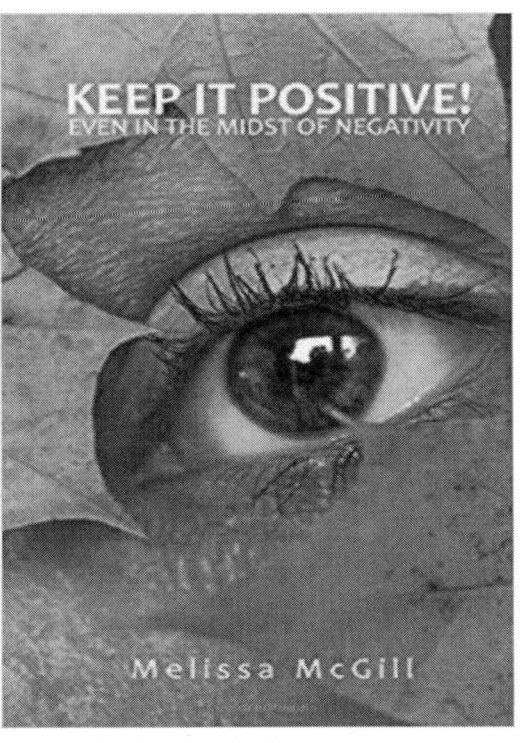

Finding Gracie

By Grace Sanchez

Grace Sanchez was born to immigrant parents, in Compton, California. She always struggled to excel and to be the best at everything she did. Grace became a wife, a mother, and a successful career woman, yet deep within she harbored a secret.

Finding Gracie reveals Grace's secret and shares her journey of personal growth and self-discovery! This inspirational book serves as a devotional and a journal to help you along your own journey of personal growth!

Soul Good Daily Devotions

By Nicole Miller

Soul Good Daily Devotions is filled with words that will captivate your mind like food does to your taste buds. This book offers encouragement, garment of praise, words of wisdom, inspiration, and food for thought. Are you ready to eat?

Nicole put this book together carefully, with love, beauty, and faith. Get ready to be fed and have your soul encouraged for 31 days. It's not just good, it's *Soul Good*!

Delayed Not Denied: The Story of Torie

By Latonya Littlejohn

She was born with what the world calls birth defects. As an infant, she was given up for adoption. The Doctors placed limitations on her that she would overcome.

In this powerful testimonial, Torie shares her journey of finding and meeting her biological family, while seeking to find her place and herself. Follow the journey of Latonya Littlejohn, also known as Torie, who was delayed, but not denied!

Books by the Lead Author

Depths of Her Heart

By Tanya DeFreitas

This poetry compilation takes you on a journey that explores the innermost & hidden thoughts, feelings, fears, and hopes of the authors. This is a collaboration project that was birthed with the intent to give women poets a platform to share their gift.

Featuring Chavonne Hurdle, Colette Toomer Cruz, Cynthia Jones, Katrina McCaleb, Lazetta Stewart, Melissa Brown, Natasha Robinson, Olivia J. Mack, Paige Taylor, Sarah Lavender, Staci Watkins, and Tanya DeFreitas, the words in the pages of this book are songs that only some can hear and understand. The melodies in this book sing about love, hurt, joy, freedom, and much more. Step into the *Depths of Her Heart*!

You Talk Too Much:
A Wife's Guide to Becoming a Silent Warrior

By Tanya DeFreitas

What is it like being married to you? Are you operating in your role as a suitable helper? Are you respecting your husband as the Bible advises? Are you praying for him? Are you helping him? Or are you hindering him?

You Talk Too Much: A Wife's Guide to Becoming a Silent Warrior is about the power of being quiet and using prayer to transform the marriage relationship. With love and grace, Tanya DeFreitas shares practical insights and her experience of learning to keep her mouth shut. In this book, you will learn how to be intentional with your words so that you too can see God move miraculously in your marriage.

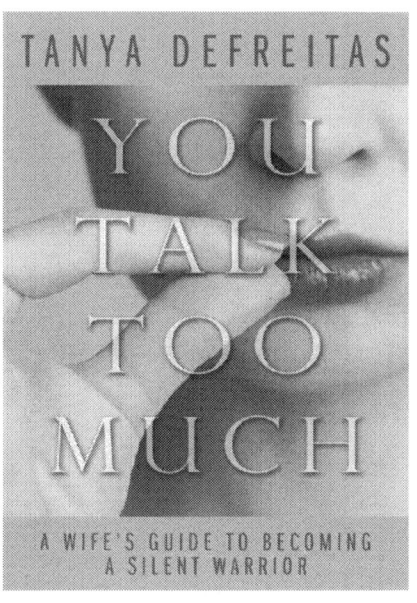

Live Your Dream Now

By Tanya DeFreitas

Live Your Dream Now is a blueprint to show you how to make your dream come true. In this captivating testimony, Tanya DeFreitas shares her journey of taking a dream she held since childhood and the process she took to make her dream a reality. This book provides five steps to help you manifest and live your dream, now!

Tidbits: 31 Days of Empowerment & Inspiration

Are you ready to be empowered and inspired? *Tidbits: 31 Days of Empowerment & Inspiration* is filled with purposeful, quick-witted nuggets of wisdom and information to inspire you to greatness! These bite-sized nuggets are simple, easy to intake and digest. Over the course of 31 days, you're given just enough to stimulate your senses and not too much to overwhelm your thoughts.

Book Club Discussion Starters

1. How many times is the word "*Pretty*" in this book?

2. How many times is the word "SAD" in this book?

3. Do you think the co-authors realized they were using the title in their actual stories?

4. What does the title, "*Pretty* SAD" mean to you?

5. Which story stood out the most to you and why?

6. Which story can you relate to and why?

7. Did any of the stories trigger any emotions of sadness, anger, or hurt within you?

8. Were any of the stories difficult for you to read? If so, which one(s)?

9. Were any of the stories inspirational? If so, which one(s)?

10. Do you have a story that is untold? If so, has this book inspired you to tell your story?

Made in the USA
Columbia, SC
01 July 2019